ENERGY, SPIRIT & HOMOSEXUALITY

THE METAPHYSICAL JOURNEY
OF A PSYCHIC

NAN MOORE

WITH

JAMES DANIELS

CONTRIBUTING AUTHOR

FRINGE-DWELLER PUBLICATIONS, LLC

Energy, Spirit & Homosexuality: The Metaphysical Journey of a Psychic

© 2009 by Nan Moore and James Daniels.

ISBN 978-0-9853819-0-5

1. Energy and Spirit 2. Homosexuality 3. Metaphysics 4. Psychics
I. Moore, Nan II. Title

Library of Congress Control Number: 2012939929

Printed in the United States of America

FRINGE-DWELLER PUBLICATIONS, LLC.
P. O. Box 626
New Vienna, Ohio 45159

Mission Statement

Make known unusual works by rare individuals who dwell on the innovative fringe of new and uncommon ideas, processes and devices.

DEDICATION

To all Souls who are searching, especially for Tony and Paul, who light the path and will greet me when I make the beautiful journey back to the light!

But the wisdom that is from above is first pure, then peaceable, gentle, and easy to be intreated, full of mercy and good fruits, without partiality, and without hypocrisy.[1]

James 3:17

FOREWORD
James Daniels, contributing author

Throughout my life, I have been fortunate to meet some of the most gifted psychics in America. Among these is Nan Moore, the author of this book. I consider her one of the most talented clairvoyants I have ever met. She is a treasured friend and teacher and I have been learning from her for over thirty-two years. She is the rare individual whose life is a living example of what she teaches. Her life's work has been a gift to thousands of souls—especially those who have exhausted the more traditional sources in their search for help.

Many of us go through life trying to figure out the nature of our existence, wondering why things happen to us and how to overcome life's challenges. The information from Spirit, as channeled by Nan Moore, presents a unique picture of our human and spiritual potential. She reveals the nature of our human and spiritual evolution clearly and simply with numerous examples of how we can increase our own understanding.

As you read her book, you will share the author's quest and thirst for truth including her unusual childhood and family experiences, brutally honest past-life revelations and plans for a future life. However, this book is much more than a story of her unusual life. Within these pages, you may acquire an understanding that could literally change your life.

The highlight of Nan's book is the groundbreaking channeled-information that reveals why people are bisexual, homosexual and trans-gendered. She writes about sexual orientation from a viewpoint of energy, Spirit and soul memories. As the ill treatment of these groupings are ever-present in the news, circumstances call for a bold, new look at time worn problems brought on by a lack of understanding and compassion for others.

INTRODUCTION
Nan Moore, author

I have been communicating with Spirit for decades in this lifetime. This has allowed me to clarify my own beliefs, give readings, explore past lives and has blessed me with many teachings—teachings that have educated and enlightened me; therefore, allowing me also to teach others. This book is about those blessings. It is a reflection on my spiritual journey which, I hope, will enlighten and bless you as it has blessed me.

There never was a time since I was old enough to think for myself, that I did not question. When something did not feel right in my gut, I would think to myself, "No, I don't believe that. There is something more, but what?"

That is the reason for this book. It is a story of questioning, searching, and finally, receiving some truths and insights to these questions. I never accepted as total truth everything I read, heard or received. I would always say to myself, "I will accept what I can for now and put the rest on a shelf in my mind." Some day, when more truth comes to me, I will sift through all this, keep what feels good, and discard the rest.

You may take the liberty to do that with this book. Do not accept it all. Take what you can and put the rest on a shelf in your mind and someday you can sift through it and toss away what you cannot accept and keep what you can. For now, this is where I am. I want to share with you my level of understanding about the path I am traveling. It is my hope that the information I offer will bring to you all that it has for me—*peace, light* & *love!*

TABLE OF CONTENTS

TABLE OF CONTENTS (continued)

PART ONE

THE METAPHYSICAL JOURNEY OF A PSYCHIC

author, Nan Moore

Spirit - the all knowing and motivating power of God that is in all things.

(A power often channeled through messengers such as psychics, prophets and the like).

soul - the individualized spark of God with all of its accumulated experiences.

spirit(s) - disembodied souls.

[Generalized definitions by the authors]

1
GIFTS

Psychic Gifts

Some called my grandmother an angel because she could find lost objects and animals. She said instead, "the angels were with her." My mother had the gift also, but not as developed as my grandmother's ability. She could find lost items. She was able to stop the pain of burns and take away warts or sties with a prayer while touching and turning her wedding ring on the afflicted area.

I believe everyone in my family was psychic but they did not then use the word "psychic." They had insights about the supernatural but they did not acknowledge psychic happenings as such.

I also believe what we learn we take with us. When we develop our psychic gifts in one lifetime, our abilities stay with us and we can build on our acquired talents in future lives. Yes, we live more than one lifetime or incarnation on Earth!

Before our birth, we search for families on Earth with a genetic predisposition that matches our own psychic and spiritual developmental level. It is not a case of choosing to be psychic in one's next lifetime and automatically coming back with that psychic gift. We must first have developed the gift in previous lifetimes.

This is very true in my own family; they definitely had a genetic predisposition for psychic gifts. Even though my mother and grandmother were psychic, my grandfather did not express any particular belief in psychic gifts. Yet, he was willing to have my grandmother help him deal with spirits materializing around him.

Many times, after my grandfather would lie down on his leather sofa, a female apparition would appear before him. In an effort to stop this from happening, my grandmother had the house blessed by a priest, lit candles and prayed constantly but the apparition did not go away.

The apparition would manifest by coming out of a yellow pillow that my grandmother had placed on the sofa. My grandmother tried throwing the pillow away; but by the time she returned to the room, the pillow would appear back on the sofa. Finally, she burned the pillow and the apparition stopped appearing.

At First Sight and Sound

My first psychic experience occurred when I was a little girl. We lived in a house that some might call a haunted house. The words we used then were "haunted" and "ghostly." I now know the word "spirits" best describe the visitors in my childhood home. Perhaps the house was haunted, but in a good way. Living in a so-called haunted house seemed perfectly natural to me and I personally do not remember being frightened.

Spirits with musical natures visited our house from time to time. The piano in our parlor started playing music very late at night. Although not discordant, the music was loud and woke us from a sound sleep.

When this first occurred, my sisters and I rushed to the railing at the top of the stairs and looked down into the parlor at the keys moving up and down on the piano. We could see the keys moving but no one was there physically moving the keys. We were simply dumbfounded!

However, upon hearing the loud music, my father tromped downstairs armed with a shotgun expecting to find an intruder. Instead, he found only the noisy piano and no intruder in sight.

He thoroughly inspected the working parts of the piano and was unable to find out why this was happening. Nothing he attempted to do up to this point was working. The fact was, the keys were moving and music was coming from a non-player piano.

Eventually, my father grew tired of the many abrupt awakenings caused by the sounds. He moved the piano outside and did some serious damage to it with an ax, as he destroyed the keys and soundboard. We were certain that the sounds would not disturb us again.

The next morning we were eating breakfast while looking out the window at the ruined piano. Quite suddenly, the broken wires of the piano began to vibrate, dance around and make sounds! Once again, we could see parts of the piano moving and we could hear the music. Then, we fully realized this was no ordinary occurrence, or some kind of prank.

We Shall See What We Shall See

I recall that my grandmother had more out-of-the-ordinary occurrences taking place in her home than we did in ours. Besides the lady appearing from the pillow, there were other spirit apparitions. Sometimes objects would move of their own accord, like small tables and chairs. Lights would go on and off and doors would open and close seemingly of their own will.

When I was about the age of ten, I saw what appeared to be a woman in the window of an upstairs bedroom at the front of our house. I was with about eight other people when I witnessed this. At first, I thought she was a visitor in our house because none of us recognized her. She had very attractive features and it was easy for us to spot her because of her long flowing auburn hair. She appeared to be talking to someone in the bedroom.

We could not account for how she entered the house without us seeing her enter. We all ran into the house and quickly leapt up the stairs and filed into the bedroom one by one. We looked in the bedroom and elsewhere upstairs; the lady could not be found. To our amazement, there was no one there except for my young nephew lying in his crib.

Another time, my teenage sister was home alone shampooing her hair in the upstairs bathroom. She thought she saw a strange man walk by the bathroom in the hallway. She peered around the bathroom doorframe and saw the stranger disappear before her very eyes. She fled from the house screaming with water dripping from her hair as she ran. This event so unnerved her that she would not stay at home alone after that.

Over time, I learned that similar events occur in the homes of other adolescent children. We were quite poor and our lives were often bleak and at times downright gloomy. Now as I reflect back to this time, I believe the spirits visited us to console and cheer us up.

I am convinced that spirits appear all the time to children, especially those with more developed psychic abilities. Compared to most adults, it is easier for children to discern Spirit's attempts to lift up their energies.

In addition, young children play freely and happily with spirit children until adults insist on telling the children that spirit children do not exist. That it is only "make believe." When children try to share stories about their spirit children friends, the adults are prone to tell the children that they just have an over-active imagination.

This pressure on the children to conform makes it difficult for children to believe in what they are actually seeing and experiencing. What a shame for the children since they derive much comfort and satisfaction from the companionship of the spirit children.

At no time do I believe the spirits who visited our homes meant us any harm. All of these experiences helped us to become more aware. I now believe the strange occurrences in my family's homes were Spirit's attempts to awaken us psychically.

Inherently, we are all psychic to one degree or another and can develop our own innate abilities. *To me it is a "natural" phenomenon to be psychic. It is actually "unnatural" not to be psychic!*

My First Reading

I was about fifteen when I went to my first "psychic" reading. At that time, I did not even know or use the word "psychic", but I had heard about a lady who told fortunes. She was a very old lady in my neighborhood who lived alone. Because all this was unfamiliar to me, I was frightened about the prospect of having my fortune read. However, I made an appointment and went to her home for a reading.

When I entered her house, I was so scared that I almost turned around and left. Yet I was curious, even though such interest or curiosity was not acceptable within the framework of my family's religious beliefs.

The reader asked me to sit in a chair facing her and, shortly thereafter, began making the sign of the cross on my forehead with oil. She told me to open the Bible to a page at random. She read a passage from the pages that fell open, tilted her head back to relax and then the pupils of her eyes rolled upward almost out of sight. The way her eyes looked really frightened me because I imagined she might perform some kind of voodoo or witchcraft on me. Instead, she sat there quietly, and then carefully and patiently began to talk to me.

She told me about my grandfather whom I had loved very dearly. I loved him more than I loved any other man. She described him to me and told me exactly how he died. Then, she said he was standing right behind me. I turned around to look and she said that I would not be able to see him. Not only did I see him, but my grandfather also reached out and touched me!

His sudden appearance surprised me, but I was not frightened because he was my beloved grandfather. When I told her that I do see him, she said that I had the gift to discern Spirit and was indeed psychic. This was the first time I had heard the word "psychic."

No True End in Sight

I left her house with a new feeling and I felt more light-hearted and alive than ever before. I felt that something new was happening in my life that was exciting and wonderful. I was so happy I could have climbed to the rooftop and shouted, "There is no death! My grandfather is alive and I saw him. He smiled at me and touched me. He still exists and everything is wonderful because there is no death. The grave is not the end."

But covet earnestly the best gifts: and yet shew I unto you a more excellent way. [1]

1 Corinthians 12:31

---

psychical   pertaining to, or connected with, the human soul, spirit; or mind; spiritualistic; psychological. Also psychic.

New Websterian

intuition   instinctive knowledge or feeling; immediate perception.

New Websterian

2

GIFT EVOLUTION

The Search for Truth

The consciousness-altering experience of psychically seeing my deceased grandfather so changed my reality that I devoted the rest of my life exploring the world of Spirit. At first, I kept this experience to myself and began to search for more truths. I read every book I could get my hands on.

At the time, there were not many metaphysical books on psychic and spiritual development. As a student of truth, I was constantly trying to perceive the spiritual reality of situations. I could not go to a local library or college to learn what I wanted to know about being psychic. I had to take what money I could make and buy what books I could find.

I have been on a long journey in my search for answers and it has not always been easy. Many ridiculed and shunned me. I lost friends and even my family turned against me for a while. Some still think I am the outcast of the family or just plain different. I now say that sometimes it is a blessing to be *different*!

As an outcast, I found it impossible to gain my family and friend's acceptance. Fortunately, this freed me to drop many of the rigid beliefs others tried to force upon me. Working with Spirit through my psychic and intuitive abilities made it even easier for me to discern for myself. I decided to choose what was applicable for my own life, especially about moral, religious and spiritual teachings.

I was raised in the Catholic faith and attended Mass regularly with my family. I never got anything out of Mass. I knew and felt there had to be a better communication and connection to God. I took that thought and feeling with me into my adult life. I believe that everyone, who goes through an orthodox religion, experiences a form of brainwashing to a degree. So many religions preach guilt, fear, hell and damnation.

I vowed to myself that I would use my psychic talents to find another path, a more suitable truth for myself. I wish I could share with everyone what I have learned; when people are not ready the truth will not come to them. Each of us must find our own way.

I hope that you will find some truth and inspiration as I share my journey with you. I do not have all the answers. I do not know all there is to know because I am still searching, learning and growing. I will continue to search for truth in this lifetime and probably hundreds more. I am on my way and I want to help others into the light, which is *knowledge,* and out of darkness, which is *ignorance*.

Meditation—My Foundation

When I was growing up, there were few psychics. Those who ventured out suffered greatly. Therefore, I privately and cautiously sought better ways to discern and apply the truths in my life. If I was to be different, I would be the best *different* I could be.

From the beginning of my search, I wanted to discover what truths were out there. I knew that there had to be something besides the heaviness of fear and guilt I experienced when I resisted the early conditioning efforts from others around me.

Through my study and intuition, I already knew I had a higher self with the capacity to be beautiful, joyful, loving, peaceful, strong, truthful and wise.

Although what I had read in books was very helpful, I needed a teacher or mentor to help me figure out how to apply the truths I was receiving. I heard about a person, that I later came to know as "Doc", who at the time was teaching metaphysical classes. I decided to attend his classes to learn about meditation.

I found meditation to be a good and true foundation for contact with the higher self. Meditation opens our energies and allows our nonphysical abilities to emerge and develop. As we sit in silence and listen to our inner voice, we can feel at one with the whole universe. We might even have a sensation of having no physical body. It is in this silence, when we quiet the mind releasing all thoughts and concerns, that we allow our higher self to work through and for us.

Everything in God's creation is perfect in its original form. How we deal with the experiences that are a direct result of choices we have made, changes us from our once perfect state. As we confront life's challenges, we often fill our lives with patterns of negative thoughts and fears. Meditation allows us to shift our awareness back to absolute truth and to remember that, *there is only one truth and life, and that is the perfect life of our creator.*

Psychometry

Doc taught us not only how to meditate but how to do psychometry. Psychometry is the practice of holding an object that belongs to someone else and tuning into or sensing the owner's vibration or energy. I discovered that anyone could do this. This practice involves energy. Everything is *energy*. What we think, say and do is energy. Energy cannot die. We can change it, but we cannot destroy it.

When we touch an object, we not only leave our DNA stamp on that object, but also leave our energetic pattern within the object. Our energy or vibration becomes forever a part of whatever we touch. Psychometry is about sensing the unique energy or vibration of a person, place or thing, and then channeling the appropriate information from Spirit, after we request it.

Psychometry helps students or psychics to lock onto a particular vibration. Many times before psychics begin a reading, they will want to hold in their hand a personal item belonging to the client. This practice helps link them to the vibration or energy of the person receiving the reading.

Once students or psychics reach a high degree of proficiency with psychometry, they can develop their skills to the point that they will be able to tune into the vibration of a person's name, voice or picture. Again, this is possible because everything associated with or touched by a person, contains the energy or vibration of that individual.

This is how a psychic is able to do phone or distance readings without actually meeting the client in person. Psychometry is like tuning into a radio station. As we practice, we become more sensitive and capable of tuning into the vibrations of particular people, places and things.

Doc's classes were very rewarding and enlightening. I advanced quickly because I had developed a psychic predisposition in other lifetimes. After finishing his classes, I began to give readings and eventually taught my own students what I had learned in Doc's meditation and psychic development classes.

When students first become interested in metaphysics, they are usually interested in many aspects of psychic phenomena. As a beginning student, I advise them to pick just one, but no more than two areas to train in. To pick more than two areas would be overwhelming for students and their training efforts would be too scattered to reach proficiency in any given area.

At the beginning of a student's training, I strongly suggest that they use meditation as a foundation to their psychic and spiritual development, followed by specialized training in a psychic development method of their choice.

One of my former students, James Daniels, contributed Chapters 9 and 10 to this book. After he was in my classes, he chose to work with dream interpretation first and later dowsing. As for me, I continued to meditate and develop my own psychic abilities and honed my skills with clairvoyance and psychometry.

Be Careful What You Ask For

There is an old saying, "You better be careful what you ask for, you just might get it," which I have found to be very true. Prayer is the sending out of thoughts and energy and asking for the things we desire and need in our life, such as a job, love, good health and friends. For instance, if we ask for a particular job, we might get it. Initially, we may be delighted because we got what we thought we wanted.

Later, we find out the job was the worst thing that could have happened to us. We may even blame or question God as a result. We may ask, "Why did this job turn out so wrong for me?" We do not always know what is best for us, but our higher self knows.

Meditation and prayer allows us to connect with our higher self. We can ask our higher self for each and everything we need. Our higher self or soul always chooses what is best for us and never makes a mistake. The soul can see and choose correctly all the experiences we need to have in our lifetime. The soul only chooses experiences needed for our growth and will not choose the wrong experiences. The unhappy things that happen to us result from choices made by our lower human nature, or lower self.

If we are in need of a job, we should never ask for a specific job. The best way to say the prayer is to ask for the job we were destined to have. An example might be:

> "Dear God, please put me in the job I am meant to be in, making the salary I am meant to make, doing what I am meant to be doing." Then, "Dear God, please give me perfect memory so I will be in the job I am meant to be in, making the salary I am meant to make. Thank you God."

Do not doubt the workings of the higher self. When we pray in this way, we are asking for the perfect job. We will have a better outcome than anything we would have chosen for ourselves. One of my favorite Bible verses addresses the power of prayer: "Ask, and it shall be given you; seek, and ye shall find; knock, and it shall be opened unto you . . . "[2] Finally, yet importantly, when we pray for something meant for us, we must be active in seeking and finding the answers to our prayers.

Criminal Cases and Missing Persons

As a psychic, I have had some very unusual experiences. I was involved with not only private consultations and teaching individuals and groups, but also worked many years with the police to help solve criminal cases and find missing persons.

I established a solid and trusted reputation in this kind of work and, over time, worked with law enforcement from New York, Ohio, Tennessee, Virginia and West Virginia.

In one case, the police loaned me evidence from a coroner's office, a sealed bag of bloody clothing belonging to a murder victim. I used the victim's clothing to help me pick up additional information for the police to investigate.

I placed the bag of clothing on my washer and left it there for a while. I had to move the bag to the garage because the spirit of the murdered man kept staying around the energy of his bloody clothes.

Eventually, the spirit of the victim communicated to my students and me that the assailant robbed him before killing him. In addition, the spirit described the assailant, his vehicle, murder weapon and its caliber; and incredibly, the murderer's name! Armed with this information, the police quickly located the murderer.

While working with this case, I decided it would be an opportune time to use this situation as a training exercise for my psychic development class participants. I had each student go to another room, hold the bag that I had placed there, and then write down her or his impressions. They did not know what was in the bag. I did tell them it had to do with a police matter.

I intentionally did not put the names of the student psychics on the reports. I used consecutive numbers to identify the students instead of using their names. The detectives only knew the numbers on the papers that matched the responses, but not the students' identities.

After the detectives closed the case, they sent me a letter and a report that informed me of the accuracy of the students' impressions. For example, Student Number 6 got the name of two suspects and the vehicle used and Students Number 1 and 8 picked up the caliber of the gun. The report detailed the hits and misses of the students' psychic impressions and helped me determine the level of their development. Thereby I could then fine-tune any future instruction.

This criminal case was an interesting and unusual experience for my students and me, but it was most unpleasant. The case was a little scary because, at that time, the murderer was still at large. In most criminal cases that psychics work on, the criminals are still running around free. There is always a great risk for the psychic, should the criminal find out the psychic's identity.

In another criminal case, my daughter and I went to a store where the murder of a woman had taken place. The murderer had removed the victim's body from the murder scene. The police needed help finding where the assailant had taken her body.

My daughter is very psychic as well and she wanted to help the police look for the murdered woman's body. We signed in at the police command center that was set up for this case. We obtained an object belonging to the murdered woman so we could tune into her energy or vibrations. Guided by our psychic impressions, we drove to a nearby cornfield to where both my daughter and I felt the assailant had taken the victim's body.

I pulled over to the side of the road and my daughter got out of the car and walked some distance into the cornfield. Suddenly, the hair on the back of my neck stood up. I sensed danger and immediately attempted to transmit a telepathic warning for her to get out of there! However, I started to panic; so I, instead, honked the car horn repeatedly to alert her to come back. In a flash, she ran back, got into the car, and said, "Mom, I know she is there. I didn't go in far enough but I know she is there."

The police had been following us by helicopter and spotted the victim's body about twenty to thirty feet from where my daughter had stopped in the cornfield. They established the identity of the body shortly before we arrived back at the command center to report our findings.

We described details of the murder to the police even the type and color of the murderer's vehicle. Shortly thereafter, they caught him. This was definitely a scary situation. We were involved in the case only a few hours after the murder had been committed.

In another case, my daughter-in-law and I helped law enforcement find a missing child in a neighboring community. My daughter-in-law was also psychic, but she did not work with her gift at that time. She asked me to help the police. I said no, but told her I would give her information about the missing child and she could be the go-between.

As I connected with the energy of the missing child, I saw dark murky water in a depression in the ground where the foundation of a building had once been. The place looked abandoned and the surrounding area overgrown with shrubs and bushes. I saw men putting the little girl's body into the water. I further related that from the missing girl's house, one could just about see this place.

My daughter-in-law called the police and described what I had seen psychically. This description helped the police to pinpoint the exact location. The murderers had stuffed the little girl's body into a dark colored plastic garbage bag and dumped it in a pit of water there. The police found the body the same day my daughter-in-law gave them my psychic impressions about the murder.

Although we wanted to help locate the little girl for the police, the circumstances of the little girl's death made us very sad. She had lost her life at such a young age and had experienced a gruesome death.

I only worked on such dangerous criminal cases on the condition that the police detectives agreed that my students, my family and I would remain anonymous. I did not want any harm to come to anyone because of my involvement.

After working with the police for many years, my husband wanted me to stop doing this type of psychic work. He had felt all along it was too dangerous and might jeopardize not only just me but also anyone remotely connected to these cases.

I, too, gradually realized working on such cases was not for me. Criminal cases tended to lower my energy. I finally agreed with my husband and stopped my involvement. After that, I was able to maintain a higher level of energy.

I continued to use prayer and meditation to balance my energies, which enhanced my psychic abilities as well. Everything that we do to build a higher consciousness stays with us throughout our lifetimes. The positive energy we create always comes back to us later on. As we connect to our higher self and realize we have unlimited potential, we are better able to improve our lives. Each of us can receive help through our intuition and psychic gifts.

Every thought we have and every word we speak creates energy that affects our lives. It is through the human mind that we create circumstances here on Earth. Our mind is an instrument, a conduit, through which we find the inner voice of the higher self or what I call the "Spirit within."

When we listen to our inner voice, we will create circumstances that never contradict the wisdom of God or the universal source. That inner voice guides and directs us to say and do those things that make us happy and whole beings. When we are not listening to that inner voice, our words, thoughts and actions are still affecting our lives. However, we may not care much for the results.

Spirit Mentor—Channeling

While we are here on Earth, we can receive helpful information through our higher self from spirit mentors and guides. I have had many helpers in my quest for truth and knowledge, helpers that reside in the nonphysical world.

The core of the information in this book, *Energy, Spirit and Homosexuality*, came through me from a spirit mentor by the name of Jean Paul. When I relate my encounters with Jean Paul to others, I generally refer to him as the "Frenchman." Nevertheless, in the book I call him Jean Paul.

Jean Paul is what psychics might refer to as a "spiritual entity." Communication from spiritual entities is one of the many ways through which a higher consciousness comes to us in the physical world.

As my gifts continued to develop, I started to receive and channel more advanced information from him. The information that flowed through me from Jean Paul and other spirit helpers not only guided me in my own spiritual growth, but also transmitted knowledge that would help others.

The initial contacts with Jean Paul began in 1979. At first, I did not know much about him personally. All I knew was that he had lived one lifetime in France in the 16th century and when he appeared before me, he assumed the appearance and personality of a person of that time.

When I received information from him, I want to assure you that I was not receiving information direct from God. Jean Paul transmitted knowledge from a group of spiritually advanced beings wishing to raise the consciousness or vibrations of those on Earth. To me, Jean Paul is a gifted spiritual mentor and guide. Not only was he my mentor and guide but also over the years, he became a very trusted friend and an invaluable source of information.

I communicate with him, as an entity from the spirit world, in much the same way as I communicate with trusted mentors in the physical world. There is little difference in my communication except that a physical mentor speaks directly to me and the spiritual mentor uses telepathy or imagery to convey the messages.

When I feel his presence (vibration) around me, it is one of patience and kindness. Many years passed before I built up trust in my channeling work with Jean Paul. When I finally turned this matter over to God, Jean Paul was able to help me express my inner knowing by encouraging me to write. I started to write some simple poems at first, then more, later on.

I was always saying to him, "No, no" or "I do not think so" when he appeared before me, asking me if I would be willing to write. I told him I was a psychic not a writer and that I did not know how to write. Although I doubted my ability to write, I began to act on faith and to record what I was receiving from Jean Paul and my other helpers.

I thank him for his patience and perseverance because I now know he was right. It later dawned on me why it was crucial that I begin to write and record what I was receiving. Spirit let me know through Jean Paul that I would write a book using the Spirit promptings and recordings of material I received from my guides—in fact, this very book.

Going a Different Direction

My journey has not always been easy, but the many revelations I continue to receive along the way, fill me with awe. Initially, family and friends rejected me; later many others I encountered shunned me, because of my emerging psychic gifts and my evolving metaphysical and spiritual beliefs. They were irreconcilable to my new way of life. I became an outsider, perceived as odd and different and avoided.

When this happened to me, their reactions hurt me deeply. Eventually, I realized that they did not have the *awareness* to understand how my gifts and beliefs had helped me to become a more giving and compassionate person. That within the depths of my soul emerged a knowingness and concern for all souls regardless of their education, gender, nationality, race, religion, sexual orientation or social standing.

One of my early challenges was to reconcile the moral and religious teachings from my childhood to those I now found so captivating. When I was younger, it was apparent to me that there was a definite line drawn between those who believed God created us and the ones who believed otherwise. I was uneasy about the open and frank discussion of such topics.

In Doc's classes, we talked about evolution. Even though the class emphasis centered on the spiritual evolution of humankind, the other information on how we physically came to be challenged my fundamental beliefs.

I became very confused at the time, as my early religious training was ever constant in my thoughts. The evolution of humankind became the greatest challenge to my belief system at that time.

An Angel Appears

One day after debating about evolution with someone in my class, I had a startling vision. In the vision, an angel materialized before me. The angel stated emphatically, "*You worry so much about evolution, did it ever occur to you that God created evolution?*" The angel then said, "*God created everything good and God created evolution. God also created the evolutionary path of your soul!*"

🕊 *It is sown a natural body; it is raised a spiritual body. There is a natural body, and there is a spiritual body.* [1]

1 Corinthians 15:44

---

evolution   development or growth; the gradual development or descent of forms of life from simple or low organized types consisting of a single cell.

New Websterian

creation   the act of creating; the thing created; the universe.

New Websterian

3

EVOLUTION AND SOUL MEMORY

Angels Go Astray

I came to believe what the angel in my vision had said, God created evolution. According to Spirit, God created all souls (angels) at the same time. In the beginning, all souls were angels and were perfect, pure spirits or sparks of the universal source.

There are many life forms within the Earth plane and our universe. Scores of people throughout time claim that extraterrestrials have visited the Earth in unidentified flying objects or UFOs. I believe God created all forms of life and extraterrestrials are just the evolutionary forms that evolved from angels outside the limits of the Earth plane.

All angels possessed the creative power of God and freewill choice. Souls had choices about where they could go and what they could do. Earth is just one tiny speck in the universe of God. Some souls chose to exist in the physical realms, some in nonphysical realms.

Exercising their free will, many angels or souls projected their consciousness into the life forms of Earth, including animals. At first, they were like children playing adventurous games.

They did not use their freewill and energies wisely and found themselves entrapped in the life forms of Earth. This entrapment in physical form lowered their ability to perceive higher states of consciousness and they lost memory of their true spiritual nature.

> **soul**   spiritual, rational, and immortal part in man; reason or intellect; conscience; life; essence; moving or inspiring power   New Websterian

The Path of the Soul

At this point, these earthly souls were only into their physical nature.   As they evolved more and more into Homo sapiens or humankind, they possessed both intelligence and a conscience and became aware of the distinct law and order of all forms of life on Earth.

Reincarnation was a creation that afforded us a means of returning to our perfect state. Reincarnation is not a belief, philosophy or religion—it is a fact that our soul is reborn repeatedly in new bodies and has experiences that will help us to remember and know our true nature and heritage.

It will take many lifetimes of experience for us to remember our full spiritual nature.   Throughout the book, I will refer to this knowingness or soul experience as *soul memory*.

With this newly given soul memory, we, the entrapped souls, were supposed to get past our lower selves. Most of us did not listen and this created negative energies or karma. With our free will, we made inappropriate decisions and our resulting choices created karma.

Good karma results from using our energies to honor and uplift all living things; this action brings positive experiences to our lives. As perfect sparks of God, we are supposed to be doing something good and positive with our free will and creative abilities.

We gradually drifted farther away from our pure potential, our higher self, and evolved toward a more material, physical nature that I will call our "human nature." Generally, we are ninety-eight percent human nature and only two percent spiritual nature.

We have all but forgotten our spiritual heritage and soon could have no memory of spiritual law and the order of things. With a renewed focus on our spiritual nature or higher self (our connection to the universal source or God), we could receive the guidance we need to accelerate our evolution.

Shape Shifting

Working with Spirit made it possible for me to realize who I am, where I came from and what I am doing here on the planet. I began to have vivid and detailed memories of my past lives.

One way our soul evolves on Earth is by recalling past life memories. This process brings the memory to the conscious level and we become aware of our true potential and learn how best to treat others and ourselves.

Each lifetime allows us to learn lessons that build on the spiritual progress achieved in previous lives. The lessons learned are stored as soul memories and are available to us. With each positive step forward, we earn the right to learn more. Our spiritual growth depends on lessons learned in the experiences we have encountered in this life and previous lives.

It would be too overwhelming to have all knowledge available to us at one time. While in the physical body, the soul is incapable of housing such as vast consciousness. However, there are still many mysteries left to us while the soul is in the physical body. When we are ready for the next layer of our understanding, the knowing will be there.

Even when we die and go to the nonphysical realm, we will not know all the secrets or all the mysteries of the universe. Death is just another step in our evolution.

In most cases, the soul of a deceased person moves smoothly to the next stage in their evolutionary path. Occasionally, the transition after death does not go so smoothly.

> **ghost** the spirit of a deceased person; apparition; the soul; breath of life; shadow New Websterian

Earthbound Spirits

People freak out when something unusual is happening in their homes. Sometimes undesirable spirits or ghosts will turn lights on and off, move furniture and become an utter nuisance.

Those who call me for help think the worst possible scenario is happening. When I go to their homes, I find the underlying cause of things very quickly and clear out undesirable influences. In over thirty years of helping people, the disruptive influences in their homes have never turned out to be demons or evil entities.

There are some useful techniques to clear earthbound spirits from homes. I tell the earthbound spirits that they are no longer in their physical body, that they are now in their astral body, have not crossed over to the spirit world yet and need to go into the white light. In addition, I tell them that their friends and loved ones, who have passed on, await them in the white light.

I can usually see the astral body of the earthbound entity or soul. It looks much as their physical body did at death. It helps to use a visualization of a daisy chain of white light energy. I start at their head and twirl the daisy chain around their head, neck, chest, waist, hips, legs and finally their feet. By the time it gets to their feet, they are very submissive, joyful, and serene and make the transition readily to the nonphysical realm. They have felt the powerful energy of the light and start to remember their true origin.

Often I go to houses where the spirits of earthbound people are trying to take drugs and alcohol. Individuals, who struggle with strong addictions while in the physical world, may not make a complete transition to the spirit or nonphysical world when they die. Such earthbound spirits are very reluctant to leave their addictions.

Teenagers and others, who are smoking, drinking or taking drugs, may actually attract earthbound spirits who have similar desires. These spirits try to get as close as possible to the teenagers in an attempt to experience the same highs that they experienced while they were alive. It does not work. They are just pests! They really aggravate and scare people. I go and help move them into the white light or nonphysical realm.

Addictions go far beyond drugs and alcohol. People with addictive behavior associated with such things as physical possessions, power, religion or sex sometimes lack the ability to make a complete transition after physical death. The stronger their addictive behaviors are, the more difficult the transition. Once they are dead, their thoughts dwell on their addictions instead of leaving the Earth and moving to the other side. This desire may be so strong that they essentially become stuck in that thought form on Earth.

Most earthbound spirits are not consciously aware that they have left the physical body and that they are dead. This is especially true with sudden, unexpected and violent deaths such as depicted in the movie, *Ghost*. [2] Because of his sudden and unexpected death, the man in the movie was confused and disoriented.

At first, he did not know he was dead. He felt like he still had a physical body, but he was only experiencing his astral body. Although this is a work of fiction and just a movie, it closely depicts the confusion that can result from an unexpected and violent death.

When people die suddenly as in an automobile accident, the force of the accident slams their consciousness out of their body. They may ask, "Where am I, what happened?" Some refuse to believe they are dead and still long to be with their loved ones. It may take a while for them to adjust to their death. Their guardian angels try to intercede and help them make the transition. Given time, their transition usually goes smoothly.

Occasionally, the earth-bound spirits' desire to remain on the Earth is so strong that it blocks the gentle nudging of their guardian angels. Sometimes, their loved ones or friends see the energetic form of the earthbound spirits because their consciousness remains so close to them. At this point a psychic or loved one can explain to the spirits that they have died and need to move on to the nonphysical world.

Some earthbound spirits are very helpful and are almost like guardian spirits. They seem to stay around the Earth plane in order to protect the living. A coworker of a friend had stopped to look at antiques for sale at a rural farmhouse. While she was looking at the antiques, the owners of the farm told her the following two stories about a male spirit or ghost living in their house:

One night the ghost had actually awakened them and communicated to them that their house was on fire. The owners got out of bed and quickly put out the fire. On another occasion, their son had come home to see them and decided to stay overnight. He had driven his motorcycle and parked it outside of the house.

Again, the ghost conveyed another warning to the owners, this time about someone trying to steal their son's motorcycle! They followed up and looked out their bedroom window and someone was trying to take the motorcycle. They immediately called the sheriff who caught the thief, thanks to the help of the ghost.

Another customer stopped by the same farmhouse to purchase antiques and the owners told the customer about the ghost living there. The customer told the owners that she had successfully removed ghosts from other dwellings and would be glad to help remove their ghost. Her statement alarmed the owners. They did not want the ghost to leave; the ghost had never harmed them and had always looked after them!

Eventually, this ghost will want to move on. However, freewill exists on a nonphysical level as well as the physical and the ghost might stick around for a while more.

People, who have gone through the dying process slowly, are very aware they are physically dead. While they are dying, their consciousness moves back and forth between the physical and nonphysical worlds. This helps smooth the way after death. Death is just a transition to another state of being.

My spiritual mentor says that ninety-nine percent of us make the transition in a good way. Most of us experience no confusion and go right through the so-called tunnel experience into the light. It is not actually a tunnel but it seems like a tunnel with bright light. It is actually a kind of portal between the physical and nonphysical realms.

After death, most of us are aware that we have died and most of us are very much relieved that our incarnation is over. We know that we are going to a better place. For our loved ones and friends that remain on the Earth, our deaths cause much grief.

Death and Grieving

Grief counseling is a major aspect of my psychic and spiritual ministry. I often provide grief counseling for clients who are dealing with the loss of a loved one. Most have never been to a psychic. Many come to my door because of their inability to deal with their loss. They usually do not know that death is only a transition and that their departed love ones continue to live on in the nonphysical world.

Grief and bereavement counseling provides spiritual fulfillment for my soul and a much needed service for the client. During consultations of this type, I explain what death is really like and what actually happens to those who have died on Earth.

This information alone is usually not enough to stop clients from grieving. To help the grieving, the departed one usually gives me a message and relays to me personal information that only the client and the loved ones could know.

Then, the client realizes that the information given in the consultation is true and confirms for her or him that their loved ones live on. It is at this point that the energy of the grieving lessens for the client. They realize that the loved ones still exist after death and will greet them again later on.

After death, the energy of our soul coupled with the energy of our guides and angels is usually strong enough to resist the grieving of our loved ones still on Earth. Most of us make the transition at death without any problems or delays. In some cases, the grieving is so severe that it prevents loved ones still on Earth from moving on with their life and interferes with the normal death transition of the departed.

A companion service hired a friend of mine named Moncie to stay with a client who had tried to kill herself. Her husband had died the year before and she had been grieving all that time to the point of not wanting to live. She had been praying for God to take her life.

Before her husband's death, the woman had been a dancer and both her husband and she had loved to dance. After his death, she stopped dancing, never went out and developed an abnormal fear of germs. This behavior continued on and on and the client often talked about wanting to die. Throughout this time, Moncie would tell the woman all the good reasons why she should want to live but this seemed to have no effect at all in diminishing her wish to die.

Then, one day everything changed. She met Moncie at the front door, grabbed and hugged her and said she had wonderful news:

The night before while resting on her bed, her husband suddenly appeared before her, walked over to her bed, sat down beside her and cuddled her in his arms. He told her that he loved her and would see her again after her life was over, but first she had much more living to do and she would be happy again.

Then, he cautioned that her grieving was preventing him from developing and doing what he was supposed to be doing. He told her that he saw her going out to his grave to talk to him. He let her know that he was not there, that he was in heaven. He kissed her on her check and disappeared.

She told Moncie, "My husband was really with me, I could feel his arms around me." Then she suddenly looked skyward and yelled, "Please God, I hope you haven't listened to my prayers because I really don't want to die, not now!" In time she stopped grieving, the germ phobia disappeared and she started inviting people to her home.

There is an old Tibetan Buddhist saying that goes something like this: "When you are born, you cry and the world rejoices. When you die, you rejoice and the world cries." It takes brave souls to come back to Earth because of the difficulties of overcoming their lower selves and balancing energies.

When our lives are over, we are happy to be free of the Earth and the difficult lessons we have chosen to learn. However, our loved ones grieve over their loss, our death and departure.

What we have done here and how we have prepared ourselves in this life, affects our life in the nonphysical world after our death. There are passages in the Bible that say, we prepare a way. We are preparing a way each time we think about death. Spirit says that at our death we have helpers, angels, who come forth to take us to the other realm and that there is no need to fear death. Death is a natural process we encounter on our evolutionary path.

Our evolution here depends greatly on our use of personal energy and soul memory. We earn the right to remember what we once knew and forgot as we evolve or grow in awareness. It is all there, the courage, potential, power, strength and everything else that we need is there in our soul memory.

🕊 ***All power is given unto me in heaven and in earth.*** [1]   Mathew 28:18

---

energy internal or inherent power; vigorous operation; power efficiently and forcibly exerted   New Websterian

---

4

ENERGY AND SPIRIT

According to my spirit mentors, God created our soul (higher self), its evolutional path and the universe. And, the universe of God includes the physical and non-physical dimensions and everything in it is composed of energy.

Early in my life, I could sense a law and order in nature, not just in the birth of a child or in the change of seasons. I just knew that there had to be more than just surface appearances. I had a relentless desire to know more about the utmost causes and underlying nature of things.

Universal Laws and Principles

After delving deeper into my metaphysical studies, Hermes Trismegistus, a contemporary of Abraham, appeared to me in a vision. He indicated that I should study the Hermetic Principles for a better understanding of the intricacy of universal laws and principles.

After much study, I now believe an understanding of these laws and principles can bring a greater understanding of the nature of energy and help us to balance our energies while we are here on Earth.

I found that although matter (energy) seems stationary to the human eye, it is actually moving back and forth or vibrating all the time. The only difference between our energy forms is that each moves at a different vibration.

Further, "that everything is in motion; everything vibrates; facts which modern Science endorses, and which each new scientific discovery tends to verify" which is "the *Principle of Vibration.*" [2] Not only does everything move and vibrate, everyone and everything possesses a particular frequency that is distinct from other bodies or matter.

Everything we think, say or do involves the use of energy. When our energies vibrate at a higher rate, we are able to communicate with the nonphysical world, create and evolve to a higher vibratory level. When our energies vibrate at a lower rate, we become fixed or stuck and do not evolve spiritually.

Etched into the memory of our soul is whatever energy we created with our thoughts, words and deeds and these energies stay a part of our space. This energy affects the quality of our life, the energy fields of other souls, the Earth's environment and its other inhabitants.

It is when we communicate and receive knowledge from Spirit that we become truly aware of our energies, the energy of others, and the existence of laws that govern all of creation.

Energy and Spirit

We, souls incarnate in a physical body, are energy. As life forms, our physical bodies are the vehicles the soul occupies and uses while in the Earth plane. Behind our heart, in energy and space, lies our soul.

Before birth, at birth or just after we are born, the soul enters the physical body. Our soul goes into a kind of spiritual shell and attaches itself to an energy line behind the heart in a point of focused energy within the physical body. This is why people often say, "I love this person with all my heart." They think they are feeling with their heart.

In actuality, they are feeling this love with their soul. Because our soul is located behind the heart, we mistakenly think we are feeling this with our heart. We could get ten heart transplants and never lose our soul because it is not a physical thing.

Some refer to the energy line that connects the soul to the point of focused energy behind the heart, as a silver cord. The silver cord makes it possible for our consciousness to leave and return at night in our sleep, when we travel to non-physical dimensions. Our soul, the non-physical self, automatically leaves and has experiences in nonphysical realms.

Everyone has a silver cord that can stretch to infinity, but stays connected to our physical body while we are here on Earth. At death, an angel severs the silver cord and we pass to a non-physical plane.

Spirit has told me that we have seven bodies with the physical body being the densest. When we die, our consciousness goes into the astral body, which at first has the appearance and look of our physical body. The astral body still has some matter to it and some density, but not as dense as the physical body.

Another principle, "the *Principle of Correspondence*", infers that our souls and the laws of creation exist in all planes or realms, "as above so below and as below so above." [3] Our physical body and the six other progressively finer energy bodies serve as the carrier of the soul's consciousness throughout the different dimensions.

The more we evolve spiritually towards our creator, the more rarified our energy forms become until we are just pure light, energy and consciousness. As life forms on the Earth, we can transform and direct our energies and expressions through the guidance of Spirit by way of the soul.

While in the earthly realm, it is through the heart center or soul that we can access information and guidance concerning the known and unknown worlds. We can explore the realms beyond Earth by using techniques such as lucid dreaming, astral projection or even a technique called remote viewing. We accomplish this exploration through the projection of our consciousness and the use of our subtle bodies.

Beyond the dense physical plane, a progression of higher planes of vibration exists. As we evolve, we move on to the more compatible levels or planes of development. *The level of our development and vibratory rate determines the plane of our existence.*

Our spiritual mentors, guides, master teachers and other evolved souls exist within the higher vibratory planes. As we evolve, help and guidance is always available through them, but only if we ask!

Yet another principle is, the "*Principle of Polarity* which proposes that everything is dual; everything has poles; everything has its pairs of opposites; opposites are identical in nature, but different in degree "[4] Some examples include "positive and negative, love and hate", peace and war, higher self and lower self, birth and death and physical and nonphysical. Without polarity in the Earth plane, we would be unable to use our free will to make choices, learn lessons and evolve.

Feminine and Masculine Energy

Interestingly, "the Hermetic *Principle of Gender* sets forth that gender is in everything; everything has its masculine and feminine principles (or qualities and energies-author's note)." [5] The soul holds memory or knowledge of our lives and helps us balance our feminine and masculine energies.

Each person, whether female or male, retains different compositions of both feminine and masculine energies. These energies affect many attributes of our personality. While our feminine and masculine energies vary, so does the intensity of those qualities within each individual.

In each lifetime, *the greater or lesser measure of our feminine or masculine energies will determine who we will be bodily, emotionally, mentally and sexually.* The closer to the mid-range and the farther we move from the extreme in our energy, the happier and more fulfilled we can be. My guides tell me that we usually make changes to our energy gradually in small steps over time.

In the chart below is a listing of attributes, *commonly but not strictly associated,* with Feminine Energy (on the left) and Masculine Energy (on the right):

FEMININE ENERGY	MASCULINE ENERGY
feeling	rational
intuitive	intellectual
receptive	assertive
creative	methodical
idealistic	pragmatic
nourishing	protective

In the chart below are qualities that serve as an example of a range of an over-abundance of either Feminine Energies (on the left side) or Masculine Energies (on the right side), both expressed in an imbalanced way.

AN OVER-ABUNDANCE OF FEMININE ENERGY EXPRESSED IN AN IMBALANCED WAY:	AN OVER-ABUNDANCE OF MASCULINE ENERGY EXPRESSED IN AN IMBALANCED WAY:
non-resistant ◆--------------------➡	violent
indecisive ◆--------------------➡	combative
insecure ◆--------------------➡	predatory
maudlin ◆--------------------➡	inhumane

Since the fall of angels into materiality, an over-abundance of masculine energy has dominated our experiences on Earth. An over-abundance of masculine energy expressed in an imbalanced way leads to violent, combative, predatory and inhumane treatment of others.

Historically, our human experiences have been mostly devoid of feminine feeling and nurturing qualities. The extreme imbalance of masculine energy and the resulting behavior are the effect of decisions made from our lower selves.

Generally, if our energies are out of balance, things almost never seem to go right and we wonder what we did to create our unhappiness. When we are unhappy, we are not in control of our overall energy. We find ourselves losing control because of an over-abundance of negative energies.

Again, if we have balanced energy around us, things have a tendency to go more smoothly. We are better able to create our own present and future by consciously choosing how we want our energetic space to be.

My mentors tell me that the collective negative energy generated by human thoughts and actions is a major contributing factor to weather extremes on Earth, such as tornadoes and hurricanes, even calamities from earthquakes and volcanic eruptions.

Within, each and every, soul is a spark of God—our higher self expressed from Spirit to the conscious mind. We reflect serenity, happiness and fulfillment when we live our lives using the God consciousness. If we live our lives from our lower physical nature, we do not feel at ease, serene or fulfilled.

When we are *not at ease* within our environment or ourselves, we open ourselves to disease, poor health and conflict. The negative thoughts that we play in our mind and the ill-conceived decisions we make through our human nature or lower selves, contribute significantly to our poor health and unhappiness.

Spirit says, it is the *evolutionary destiny of the soul to balance its feminine and masculine energy.* We are here on earth so that the soul can balance its energies.

God

All souls have been striving to overcome their lower selves and not to give in to anger, envy, hate, resentment and the thoughts and behaviors that have impeded our evolution. My guides and mentors say we have not perfected our souls yet, but Spirit assures me of a patient God with an unlimited and unconditional type of love or charity.

> **charity** the disposition to think well of others; liberality; alms; universal love   New Websterian

God or the universal source's love is unconditional and never gives up on us. If God did give up on us, then his love would be conditional.

To me, the universal source is pure energy, divine love and from that spark of the divine within our soul, we can manifest great spiritual works of healing, prophecy and many other gifts.

God helps us in so many ways. He gives us lifelines in our palms to help guide us through the earth's experiences without making so many mistakes. He gives us astrology, so that the planet and stars can lead us and teach us the order of things. Numerology, so that numbers can enlighten us as to the complexity of creation and dreams so that while we are asleep, we can gather information for future decisions.

Spirit is a perfect life-giving force. We cannot take anything away from this universal source and we cannot add anything to it. This source is greater than anything we can imagine.

Still yet, another principle, the *"Principle of Mentalism"* establishes "the mental nature of the Universe" and that "we exist in the mind of God" and that the part of us which is divine makes up the world and everything in it. The universal source is the "mind of all." [6]

Everything we think, say and do is energy that becomes a part of the mind of the universal source and is stored in the Akashic Records or the great hall of records. My guides tell me that this hall of records holds all of our soul's experiences and sojourns in the physical and nonphysical planes and all past, present and future information is stored there. We can access the records through different means such as clairvoyance, hypnosis, meditation, dreams and a number of other methods.

Since everything we take in, think, say and do is energy—we (and only we) are responsible for what we allow in and send out. It pays to think good thoughts, say positive things and do things that are of a helpful nature. Remember, *like attracts like*. If we are peaceful and balanced, we receive harmonious returns. If our thoughts and actions are out of balance, we get disharmony.

Although the *Law of Attraction*, "like attracts like", is not one of the Hermetic Principles, it is highly useful in understanding how we can better balance our energies. My spirit guides tell me that the Law of Attraction is more important than any one of the immutable Hermetic Principles.

The Hermetic Principles do not vary; they are fixed and immovable. Even with our free will, we cannot change these principles. We live and exist within their *unchanging* boundaries.

On the other hand, the effects of the Law of Attraction are more fluid and are subject to our personal choices and decisions. The Law of Attraction stipulates that negativity attracts more negativity, aggression attracts more aggression and conversely—love attracts more love and compassion attracts more compassion.

We create our own reality from what we think, say and do; and how we react to the lessons we have chosen. It is imperative that we choose our words and actions carefully by always having the higher standard firmly fixed in our hearts and minds, for "like truly attracts like."

Understanding the Law of Attraction helps me personally to protect myself from negative energies, people and entities. I never watch a TV show, movie or documentary that is violent or portrays demons or evil things. If I watch negative types of shows, the energy could stay with me and I could attract that same kind of energy to me for real. I take no chances. I pay attention to what I watch, think and do.

In addition, I send out good, positive energy through ongoing prayers and affirmations. In my psychic and spiritual work, I have never had a problem with demons or evil spirits. My mindset does not attract such things. Depending on what we attract to our lives, we may be moving toward a place of supreme happiness or we may be creating our own personal hell.

No Hell?

Spirit says that there is no such thing as hell. Hell is a place created in the mind of man to control others with fear. The closest thing to a place called "hell" is our experiences here on Earth, particularly by how we treat our fellow human beings. The atrocities of the wars in the past are far worse than any hell that we could conjure up in our own minds. What hell can we visualize that is worse than the torture, mutilation and killing of men, women and children? If we see a burning hell, then we created it. God did not.

The higher self is the divine within our soul. If the soul leaves the body at the time of physical death and goes to a hell and burns, then so would the universal source, because the spark of God is within each of us.

My belief is that the source cannot die and neither can we. The divine cannot burn in a hell and neither can we. We should not listen to everything man has written or said. People wrote according to their level of understanding and they could not see the truth completely, so they distorted the oral and written truths. As time passes, we will evolve in our understanding and we will eventually know *truth*.

Death—the Transition

The only thing that "dies" at death is our physical body. The body will go back to dust either naturally or by cremation. The body is the vehicle the soul uses to get around in the Earth's dense gravitational field. Since we work out most of our lessons on Earth, we need our bodies while we are here.

When the transition of death occurs, angels sever the energy line or silver cord. The spirit or soul then leaves through the top of the head. This frees the soul from the Earth plane as it travels through a tunnel of sorts to the nonphysical realm.

At this point, we begin to look back on our latest earthly experiences and we will "feel" all the pain and suffering we have caused others. We can hardly tolerate the regret and sorrow over our harmful actions. Yes, we experience all the emotional pain we have caused others and we judge ourselves.

The universal source does not judge, only man does. If God judged us, God would no longer be the divine. According to my spiritual mentors, God is love, unlimited love, and never judges any of us.

After death we look back at our lives, review the lessons we were supposed to learn and judge ourselves far greater than anyone ever could. However, I thank the source for reincarnation and the resulting gift to be able to come back to Earth many lifetimes so I can learn and undo the harm I have done.

We can see the big picture of our past lifetimes on the other side, not only when we have passed into the Spirit (died), but also when we take a nap or go to sleep at night.

During sleep, our physical bodies are revitalized and renewed. This is why it is so important that we receive sufficient, uninterrupted and regular sleep. Our soul, however, never sleeps and it leaves the physical body through the top of our head when the physical body is asleep.

When our soul or consciousness leaves the sleeping physical body, the soul uses the less dense but higher vibration astral body to move about the Earth and into the nonphysical realms.

The soul sometimes moves out of the physical body before we are fast asleep. When this happens, we feel like we are in two different locations at once. When the soul enters the body shortly after the physical body awakens, it will feel like a sudden jerking sensation, as if the body is catching itself when falling. When the soul returns to the body, it enters through the stomach or solar plexus area. We can confirm much of this information by learning and using the process of astral projection or lucid dreaming.

The higher vibration of the astral body still has the look of our physical body but the astral body allows us to go through solid physical walls! When we die, we discard our physical body and the astral body houses our consciousness as we move away from the Earth plane.

Once we reach a Christ-like consciousness, unconditional love, charity and no negative karma as accomplished by Jesus and other ascended masters, we stop coming back to Earth. Yet, we continue to evolve towards God even in the nonphysical realms. The more we evolve, the more rarified and less dense our subtle bodies become until we are just pure energy.

Spirit says that our higher self (soul), as a spark of God, always stays a part of the universal source whether we are in a physical or nonphysical body, regardless of the state of our energetic levels.

The Lord shall preserve thy going out and thy coming in from this time forth, and even for evermore. [1] Psalm 121:8

And as we have borne the image of the earthy, we shall also bear the image of the heavenly. [2]
1 Corinthians 15:49

But I say unto you that Elias is come already, and they knew him not . . . [3]
Mathew 17:12

Marvel not that I said unto thee, Ye must be born again. [4] John 3:7

And no man hath ascended up to heaven, but he that came down from heaven even the Son of man which is in heaven. [5]

John 3:13

Reincarnation a return to body and flesh, after having left them for a more spiritual state. The possibility of Reincarnation is held by the Christians as well as by the Brahmans. [Latin]   New Websterian

Incarnation the act of clothing with, or of assuming, flesh; embodiment in human form; a striking exemplification or personification; the assumption of human nature by the Son of God [Latin]   New Websterian

---

5

REINCARNATION

The Soul Reborn

Reincarnation is the rebirth of a soul in a new body. We keep coming back to Earth until we balance our energies. Earth is a big learning center. We are the students. We come back each time with specific lessons to learn. We choose to be around certain people to learn these lessons. Sometimes we allow the desires of our human nature to distract us and do not accomplish all of the lessons we chose for ourselves. Eventually, we will remember and learn how to balance our human nature, if not in this lifetime, then in future incarnations.

About ten thousand people claim to have been Cleopatra in a past lifetime. However, most of us were not well-known kings or queens in our past lives, although it is tempting to believe that we were. We are all important regardless of our past lives because our souls are evolving and we are working through lessons to perfect ourselves.

Soul Mates and Friends

Spirit says that there are soul mates but rarely on a romantic level. We probably do not have any negative karma with our soul mate. We have already worked it out in the many other lifetimes that we have shared. We can have a variety of relationships with soul mates, perhaps as a parent, child or sibling. We will have a good rapport and we feel like we want to be with them all the time.

A soul mate can be a best friend. You may find when you are talking with your soul mate, you often finish each other's sentences. I have a best friend and we are soul mates. We have had no conflict in our relationship and share an affinity and closeness that is unlike most other relationships.

We can also have a romantic relationship with a soul mate. I would guess, based on my experiences as a psychic and in my work with Spirit, only about five percent of the Earth's populations are with their soul mates. If you do have a romantic relationship with a soul mate, you will be like best friends, communicate well and be very compatible. You will tend to put each other first and trust each other. You will also have a deep sense of being in love, which you have never experienced before.

This relationship with a soul mate is very rare. Sometimes we miss the opportunity to be with our soul mate because our human nature comes in so strong. If we slow down and connect with our higher self, we will clearly see the best choice for us in this lifetime.

Regardless, we do not necessarily need a soul mate to be happy in a relationship. The people can be happily married and not be with their soul mates. This does not mean they cannot communicate well and be compatible. They may have to strive harder than they would with partners who are soul mates, but they can still be very happy.

There appears to be times and places to meet the ones who are meant to be our life partners. Although a plan was in place before we were born, we do not always recognize the opportunity. Life on the Earth plane and our human nature can be very distracting.

When we meet someone new, our soul may tune into a vague memory from a past life. Inexplicably, a certain person attracts us and he or she feels familiar to us. This most certainly is a past life memory, but this feeling of knowing them may lead us away from the one we are "destined" to be with in this lifetime.

If we have not developed our intuition and psychic abilities to receive guidance from Spirit, finding the one meant for us will be difficult. We are here to learn life's lessons. Optimally we chose a life partner so we can help each other move forward on our respective spiritual paths.

We learn by returning to the Earth repeatedly throughout many lifetimes until we get it right. I was not married to my soul mate this lifetime. My husband and I were together because we shared lessons that needed addressed and learned.

My Son, Tony

Since current family situations often originate from past incarnations, I was curious to know why our youngest son, Tony, was neurologically and developmentally disabled. He was dependent on us for almost everything, although he could walk and feed himself.

He had trouble with speech as well as other disabilities. The skills of a speech therapist and our patience helped him surmount the many difficulties he faced, when he tried to express himself. Later on, with therapy, we could understand about eighty-five to ninety percent of what he said.

Sometimes it would take many attempts for us to understand what he was saying. He would become so frustrated and upset and because we loved him so dearly, we strongly felt those same emotions.

While meditating one day, I asked my higher self to reveal soul memories of a past incarnation involving Tony. I had the following past life recall:

I saw myself in a past lifetime, living on the western prairie land, which looked like Kansas or Nebraska. We were settlers and I was a female married to the same man who reincarnated as my husband in this current lifetime. We had seven living children then and I had lost three. Tony was also our son in that lifetime and born retarded. We all lived in a cramped one-room cabin with a loft.

My husband in that lifetime read from the Bible two to three times a day. Had he not believed strongly in the commandment, "THOU SHALT NOT KILL." [6] I believe he could have killed the boy without a second thought.

I, too, was just as heartless. I never bathed the little boy, never touched him. I threw him scraps of food, which he had to eat off the dirt floor.

In those days when people had retarded children, they thought of them as imbeciles. Having a retarded child then brought much shame to the family. Tony, as a little boy in that lifetime, received no sign of affection from us as his parents or his siblings.

We had several cows, one bull and some chickens and lived on a dry, dusty prairie. Food was often scarce, even water was hard to come by as the river dried up at times. We resented having to share anything with the boy but had to put up with his presence, as we felt we could not do away with him.

One unbearably hot day as I was making bread and my husband was milking the cows, I noticed the boy trying to open the gate where we kept the bull. The rope that secured the wooden gate to a fence post was frayed and old. It did not take much for him to break it and go inside the fenced area. I turned my back to the door and ignored that he might be in danger.

My husband also saw him go into the fenced area but put his head onto the side of the cow and kept on milking. The bull charged and trampled the little boy; it was all over in a matter of minutes. I heard a few weak cries and then there was only silence.

I waited a while as my husband approached the little boy's body. I walked over to him and then asked, "He's dead, isn't he?" My husband did not answer me. He secured the bull, picked up the little boy and put him in a burlap bag.

My husband, our other children and I walked to the top of a nearby hill. The children dug a hole in the ground for a grave. My husband dropped the body into the makeshift grave and covered it over with dirt. He then took out the Bible and read a passage.

We both figured that we had not killed him. We reasoned that the bull had killed him, not us. My husband even remarked that it was "God's plan."

Tony was that little boy and he chose to come back this lifetime to help us learn compassion, patience, tolerance and unconditional love. I hope that we have learned from the past and our present experiences. Tony has been a teacher more than to just my family in this lifetime. Hundreds of people knew him and had the opportunity to grow spiritually through association with him. Some did, others did not.

Nevertheless, he knowingly suffered in this lifetime so that others could evolve. As he grew older, I realized that he was a genius in many areas and he was quite psychic. Tony had an unusual gift. As a young handicapped child, he would sit on the floor in my classes with twenty-five to thirty-five students and spin a globe of the world, stop it and predict earthquakes, hurricanes and other global disasters.

While he was telling of future events, most of my students would take notes of what he was saying. Later on in the year, they would retrieve their notes, research the events and then confirm much of what he had foretold.

He died at the age of twenty-four, went to a beautiful place and is very happy there. I feel his presence a lot. I see him at night while my physical body is sleeping and my spirit is visiting the other side.

Other souls will choose to incarnate, coming back again and again until all have learned. The Bible says, "Suffer little children, and forbid them not, to come unto me: for of such is the kingdom of heaven." [7] I believe this means that when souls, especially as a children, come to Earth and suffer greatly and die, it will be their last incarnation on the Earth.

My spirit mentors tell me that these souls have made the ultimate sacrifice. They have chosen to serve as models, to suffer and die, to provide opportunities for us to use our free will for the betterment of all and to advance spiritually.

Mother Mary and a Rose

In 1969, Mary, the mother of Jesus, appeared to me. At that time, doctors were advising my husband and me to place our youngest child, Tony, in an institution. Our four other children were not receiving much emotional attention because Tony's needs were so great. We felt the attention must go to the child that was frail and ill. This made us, especially me, feel helpless and inadequate as a mother. I could not bear to lose him and decided not to place him in an institution.

One day in that same year while I was wondering if I had done the right thing, Mother Mary appeared before me and told me that I was doing the right thing to keep our fragile son at home. I asked her, "How do I know I am really seeing and hearing you?" She replied, "I'll give you a sign." I had to ask her again, "You will give me a sign?" She confirmed that she would. I could not believe I was worthy to have this happen to me. She read my thoughts and said to me, "Everyone is worthy and special. You are doing the right thing by keeping your son at home and not placing him in an institution."

Then Mary said, "I will bring to you one of a set, one of a pair or one of a dozen if the answer is that you are not meant to place him." She had me write this down on paper, sign my name, seal the note in an envelope and place it inside a book in a bookcase. The month was January 1969. The demands of my everyday hectic life as a caregiver soon pushed the vision from my mind. I told no one, thinking they would be skeptical to say the least.

On a sunny day in May, the doorbell rang and I answered it to find a deliveryman. He handed me a rose and as I placed it on the table, Mary appeared before me once again and said, "There child is your answer!"

I hurried to the bookcase, retrieved the book that contained the paper with the signed information and took it back to the living room where I had been sitting with my husband. I asked him to open the envelope and read the note and he did so. I asked him to confirm for me what it said. He related that I was to receive one of a set, one of a pair or one of a dozen if I had made the right decision to keep Tony at home.

I had just received "One flower of a set, a rose." I then asked him, "Who does the card say the rose is from?" He replied, "The card is from *Mary*."

Mother Mary had impressed my friend, Mary, to send me a rose. I believe she timed the delivery of the flower and card to arrive in time for Mother's Day. I felt the flower both honored me as a mother and she as the mother of Jesus.

My friend, Mary, had never sent me a flower before or since then. I had my answer, my sign. After that, I never doubted again that I was doing the right thing; I then felt I had made the right decision.

Finally and more significantly, knowing about my past treatment of Tony in another lifetime (the settler incarnation in western United States) had helped me to follow through in this lifetime and not repeat the same mistakes as in that past lifetime. I had asked my higher self to open the past life memory that would help me understand why my husband and I had the burden of caring for such a severely disabled child, along with raising four other children. The past life memory that came because of my asking, left little doubt in our minds as to why we were faced with such a formidable challenge. Our current incarnation afforded us the opportunity to set right the wrongs of the past. We came to look upon this incarnation of our son, Tony, as a blessing—no longer as a burden to bear.

When people ask me about reincarnation, I usually tell them that as we study reincarnation more information will come to us. Someday, we will more fully understand the total truth. The total truth is within each and everyone. God knows everything and if God is within us, we have the potential to know it as well.

When the soul has balanced and mastered its energies, then its sojourns on the Earth plane will end. In the last incarnation of the man, Jesus, he made his *will* one with his higher self, reached a perfect state of balance and became the Master. He broke the cycle of reincarnation within the physical Earth and ascended to the nonphysical realm. His message to us was, and still is, that *we are more than just our physical bodies—we have a spiritual destiny to evolve out of the Earth plane and to return to our creator.*

KARMA

*by **Nan Moore***

What lessons do I have to learn upon this planet Earth?

Will I work it out this time or wait for a future birth?

Do I live by the Golden Rule with every soul I meet?

Or, have I taken another path of anger, greed and defeat?

Have I learned how to understand to be compassionate and sincere?

Am I honest and cheerful with those that I am near?

I hope I'm doing what I should with my time on this Earth plane,

cause if it's not right this time I'll have to do it again and again!

🕊 ***And let us not be weary in well doing: for in due season we shall reap, if we faint not.*** [1]

Galatians 6:9

🕊 ***. . . as thou hast done, it shall be done unto thee: thy reward shall return upon thine own head.*** [2]

Obadiah Verse 15

6

KARMA, FORGIVENESS AND SOUL MEMORIES

Cause and Effect

What goes around comes around is known as the *Principle of Cause and Effect* [3] or karma. From every experience we have, there is a cause and effect factor (action and reaction). This is another universal law or Hermetic Principle. Something affecting us now could be the result of an experience from either our current or past lifetimes. We go with our earthly human nature most of the time and that is why we create what some call karmic debts.

Karma is a lesson that we have to work out with another person or group of people. Generally, our positive karma enhances our future experiences and our negative karma tends to bring difficult learning lessons later on. Learning difficult lessons alleviates negative karma and enhances our spiritual growth. However, tuning into the lower self builds negative karma. We cannot evolve out of the Earth plane if we are imperfect. That is why we are constantly trying to perfect our soul.

If a drunk driver kills a child with his car, this is cause and effect resulting from his "human nature" choices, not anything that his higher self has chosen. The drunk driver has incurred much karma (debt) with this situation. He took a soul out of the Earth plane before her or his pre-destined time to go. The drunken driver will have to return to Earth many times because of his decisions and actions in that one lifetime. He will have to feel all the emotional pain he caused the child's family and friends. He will feel this just after his death occurs when he goes through his life review and must look back at his actions in that particular lifetime. Anyone who kills another has a karmic debt to work out.

My students asked why we have souls on the Earth who can kill indiscriminately and have no conscience about killing. Examples could include drive-by shooters that kill for sport, serial killers, those who commit genocide and the like. Spirit says these souls are new to the planet, to the physical dimension, not new souls because we were all created at the same time.

When a soul is first born into the Earth plane, it projects its consciousness into a physical body for the very first time and this lessens the consciousness of its connection to God. These souls have not been on this planet long enough to build up sufficient consciousness to not want to kill. The Principle of Cause and Effect over many lifetimes will balance their new human nature through difficult lessons encountered.

We work out karma and perfect our nature by remembering what we are here for and gradually move toward a higher consciousness. Master souls have done this. Eventually, they remember fully the reason for their incarnation and master the Principle of Cause and Effect. Their every action (causes) manifests positive outcomes (effects). They stop being the reactive and emotional pinballs of their environment (lower self, friends, family and society). Their mental focus becomes one of inner and outer peace, harmony and unconditional love. They mastered their energies and the lessons of the Earth plane.

Life is the ongoing process of learning to balance energy. Karma is the ongoing process of balancing life experiences (energy and soul memories) from one lifetime to the next.

Generally, of the negative things that happen to us in any one lifetime, *sixty to seventy percent is new karma and the rest is from our past lives.* Knowing this really puts a lot more responsibility on us. We, literally, create our own lives. Yet, not all experiences we have are karmic; we chose some experiences to strengthen our abilities, character and talents or to demonstrate unconditional love.

Before we incarnate, we pick life-learning situations that help us grow stronger spiritually and in our wisdom. We may even agree to enter into life situations that have nothing to do with the negative karma incurred in our past lives.

When planning our incarnations or lifetimes before rebirth into the Earth, we review many possibilities. We do not always pick the easiest path. We can make it hard on ourselves as I did with Tony, my son. I took care of Tony for almost twenty-five years, after he incarnated into my family again. Even though we both planned this before I incarnated in this lifetime, I did not have memory of this until after he was born.

Tony chose a challenging incarnation. He was willing to incarnate and suffer in order for us to learn compassion, patience and unconditional love. It was a big step for my son. He became my teacher and he evolved. Because Tony was willing to suffer, he allowed others and me to repay our karmic debts.

With regard to the events that happen in our lives, obviously not everything is the result of negative karma. Tony purposely chose to come back into a situation that was very difficult for him. For him, this was not a karmic debt situation to work out but a freewill choice.

Personally, I have worked out much karma in this lifetime brought about by the karma I caused in previous incarnations. I would say the greatest things I have learned are compassion, patience, tolerance and unconditional love. I learned all this from Tony, my son by birth, and Paul, my surrogate son, who were both here to be my teachers. That is why I dedicated this book to them.

Some ask if I chose to be a psychic in this lifetime to negate past karma. Working with my clairvoyant gift did not have anything to do with negative karma. After I was born into the Earth, I had no recall of wanting to be psychic. I just wanted to know what was out there besides conformity and indoctrination. I asked God to give me the truth in my meditations.

With meditation came my psychic awareness. Thereafter, I started to work with my abilities to help others. Only after I started working with my psychic abilities, did I find out that I had made a decision to do this work before incarnating on Earth. I was not aware before then, that I would be doing psychic work.

Some people say, "They are not going to incarnate on Earth again, because it is too hard." However, when they are on the other side in their non-physical body, they will see more clearly the need to reincarnate, if they want to progress and evolve. The desire to evolve back to God and to perfect their souls is so strong that almost all souls choose to reincarnate every chance they get.

Forgiveness

forgiveness   pardon; remission
New Websterian

I asked my spiritual mentor if there was any way to work out karma and the lessons involved with that karma without being with the person or grouping, involving the karmic debt. My spiritual mentor affirmed that it was possible but only though "forgiveness." If someone hurt and demeaned us in a past life, there would be a "cause and effect." We might carry the energy and soul memory of that "effect or reaction" into this lifetime with feelings of low self-esteem and a lack of confidence in ourselves. The way to freedom from a karmic connection is through forgiveness. Use a "forgiveness affirmation" like the one below until you achieve a sense of peace.

> **"I forgive anyone who has hurt me in any way, by something said or done to me in this lifetime or in a past lifetime. I give them my forgiveness and release them from any karmic debt they may have owed me. I give them forgiveness and permission to be free and happy.**
>
> **From anyone I may have hurt by thought, word or deed in this lifetime or any past lifetime, I ask them for forgiveness and permission to be free and happy."**

The only way to heal ourselves is through forgiveness. Forgiving the transgressions of others brings healing. Healing brings about the forgetting and the release of transgressions from our consciousness. When we have successfully forgotten all transgressions, we enter into a state of grace. A state of grace is the "free unmerited favor and love of God . . ." [4]

We are turning the other check when we forgive. Sometimes it is difficult but it is worth it. If we feel troubled and we do not know why, this means we have not worked on our forgiveness enough. We do not have to like a person's human nature, what they have done or even stay around them, but we do need to love the person's spirit. If we do not, we will not have peace and harmony in our life. Remember, *the greatest gift God has ever given us is love. The most effective tool God has ever given us is forgiveness.*

Our relationships in this life may have karmic ties to past lives. If you meditate about those closest to you, you may begin to see the lessons that are involved. In many cases, both parties have opportunities to learn and therefore grow spiritually. The lessons could involve aspects such as compassion, love, mercy, patience, selflessness and tolerance.

In the story below is one of the strongest soul memories of karma that I have memory of and involved several members of my current family:

In the 1600 or 1700s, I lived with my Native American family in a village, in an area known today as the southwestern part of the United States. We were Navajo. I was a female and betrothed to the chief's grandson, Running Water. My name translated into English was Yellow Fox.

One day when Running Water and I came back after a picnic my sister prepared (she is my oldest sister in this lifetime), there was a crowd of villagers circling around this little blond-haired white girl who appeared to be about four years old.

They were jeering at her, pushing her around, and pulling her stringy yellow hair. She was dirty all over and tears had made streaks down her face.

It was clear to me that the tribe had decided to kill her. I jumped in front of her and cried, "No, don't kill her!" The tribe was shocked at what I had just done. I did not know why I felt such a compassionate, warm feeling toward her. I only knew I did not want her hurt or killed. I begged Running Water to speak to the chief, his grandfather, and finally he did. The chief said we could keep the girl but if I chose to keep the girl, the chief would banish my mate, the little girl and me forever from the tribe.

After we left the tribe, Running Water did not speak to the child or me for about a year after that. Gradually, the girl won his heart. She already had stolen mine the minute I saw her. We named her Yellow Water after both of us. She made us laugh when we thought we would never laugh again.

Ostracized from the tribe, we kept moving to the northeast. We lived on bugs, snails, snakes and worms. When we could find a cave, Running Water would snare a rabbit, sometimes a squirrel, or other small animals and we would roast it on an open fire in the cave. Those times were rare, so when we found a cave we would stay several days.

We were always on the move and heading northeast. For about four years, we moved and hid from the white men and other Native Americans who might be hostile to us because of the little white girl. We traveled until we reached a place currently known as Virginia.

It was late summer and Yellow Water, now eight years old, was helping me gather berries. Running Water was collecting whatever his snares had caught. I was twenty or thirty yards from Yellow Water and heard her scream before I saw what had caused her to cry out. Five white men had happened onto our camp and one had grabbed her.

Running Water ran to her defense and before he could raise his hand, he was shot at close range and fell dead to the ground.

Yellow Water was crying hysterically for Running Water and me. By then she could decipher our language and still remember English as well. She knew what the white men were saying and planning to do with her. They talked excitedly about the reward they would probably get when they returned Yellow Water to her white family.

I also knew what they were planning to do with Yellow Water. I could understand some English because Yellow Water had tutored me in the English she had once learned, before her abduction by our tribe.

One of the five white men carried her away kicking and screaming and on that day took my heart with them. I had stayed hidden in the thick brush, the way Running Water had taught us to do for survival. After the white men left, I ran to Running Water's body.

They had scalped him and the blood that ran from his body made a small stream down the hill. When I touched him, his body was already cold.

I dug a grave with my bare hands. I remember the soil was rich and damp in my hands. I made scratches down both sides of my face as I wailed, first quietly, then louder and louder. I did not care who heard me or even if I lived. My beloved was dead and my beautiful child was gone. My life was now empty and without hope.

I stayed by the side of the crudely dug grave that I had clawed out of the ground for him. I covered his body with as much dirt as I could gather. I piled leaves, rocks and sticks on top of the dirt.

After I left Running Water's grave, I stopped crying and I shut down all emotions. I began to walk out into the open, not hiding anymore. It was not long before an Indian war party came upon me. They decided not to kill me and took me back to their village.

The reason they let me live was to tend to orphaned children in their tribe; however, I was not treated with respect or dignity. Sometimes the village women even beat me.

I vowed then I would never love another human being again and I did not in that lifetime. I essentially grieved myself to death and just barely two years later, I died alone and bitter.

The child, Yellow Water, incarnated in this lifetime and is my second daughter. She knows this story and understands why she has always been afraid of losing me. She was always afraid I would move to another state and leave her. She purposely chose a college career, with transferable skills, so it would be easier for her to find employment anywhere I might move. As she grew older, she remained determined to stay with me.

Today, we have had a very close relationship. Now an independent woman, she has considered moving away from me to another state. I believe I have been able to help her overcome the fear of abandonment brought about by events that occurred in that particular past lifetime in Virginia.

My oldest son was my little Navajo brother in that same lifetime. White men had killed him while he was out on a territorial scouting mission with other Navajo warriors. He was only fifteen years old when he died.

No one ever told me the story of Running Water, Yellow Fox and Yellow Water. I meditated for quite some time and recall vivid soul memories from that lifetime. After receiving the information, I went to a local psychic who did a reading for me about that particular past lifetime. The reader confirmed most of what I had obtained from my meditations.

I have been able to recall that Running Water's grave was about a fourth of the way down from the top of Powell Mountain. Over the years, I have often thought of going there and looking for his remains.

Incidentally, the man I am married to this lifetime was born on Powell Mountain. He was one of the white men who took Yellow Water from me and he was the one that killed Running Water. In the lifetime as settlers, he was my husband when the bull killed our son, Tony.

However, in this lifetime, he has been a very good husband to me, always putting me first. He has done so many good things for me since I have known him that I have finally forgiven him for any past hurts and wrongs, ever done to me in any lifetime.

I, myself, have found it hard to forgive. It was very difficult for me to get past the soul memories, especially since my current husband was my enemy in the Navajo past life. I have struggled to stay objective and to realize that it is for the good of my soul that I must forgive again and again until I am healed. Once I have successfully forgiven another, there is a sense of serenity that fills my soul and I am able to be at peace with that person.

It may take a long time before we can truly forgive a person who has done us a great harm. Do not give up! Keep on turning the other cheek and keep on forgiving others. Believe me, it is well worth your effort because you can then experience the peace and serenity that comes from being able to forgive.

Remembering Past Lives

I can remember eight of my past lives. I can connect my past lives to the relationships of many within my current circle of family and friends. Not everyone is ready to delve into her or his past lives, but you will hear the words when the ears are ready.

I suggest that you not go straightaway to a psychic to hear about your past lives. I encourage you first, to try meditation to bring up a past life or two. All you need to do is say a prayer of protection from your highest spiritual source. Then, ask your higher self to see your most recent significant past life. Start at the age of five. Ask your higher self, questions like:

- Am I male or female?
- What part of the world am I living at in this past lifetime?
- Who are my parents?
- Is there a connection to me now in this lifetime?
- What did I look like at an older age?
- What is my vocation or work?
- What was my purpose in that lifetime?
- What karma, if any, did I incur?
- How did I die?

Try this for fifteen minutes, two or three times a week. When you draw a blank, let it go and ask to see another incarnation. Just let it flow as if you are seeing a movie. Be sure to keep a journal of everything you feel or see.

You will be surprised and amazed at how many things just come together and make sense to you. The more you are diligent in this practice, the more you will remember events and details. After you have compiled information from two or three separate lifetimes, you may want to get a psychic reading from a reputable psychic who is skilled at doing past life readings.

Soul Memory and Future Planning

I know I have been African, Native American and Egyptian in my past lives. It really does not matter to me what race or nationality I was in a past lifetime. What matters to me most is what I have learned and how close I am to attaining unconditional love for all.

In my next lifetime, I will be a female born and raised in western part of North Carolina around Ashville. As an adult, I will be around five feet nine inches tall and will not have to experience a weight problem (as I have in this lifetime).

Unlike many of my past incarnations, I will choose not to marry nor will I have children. Since I have faithfully worked through karmic situations with my current husband and children, there will be no need to incarnate with them in my next lifetime. My focus will be on the work I wish to do.

My plan is to continue to develop as a psychic and spiritual teacher. I will be formally educated with a Ph.D. in psychology and parapsychology and will teach courses at a college or university level.

My advocation during my next life will involve work with the conservation of the Pisgah National Forest, to reduce the ongoing blight of the trees there. I will finally get to live peacefully and serenely near the forest that I have grown to love over many of my lifetimes on Earth. I will also have the opportunity to share the love of someone special. My guides have informed me that my plans are appropriate and approved for my next incarnation.

In this chapter, I have given examples of personal karma, in my own life and others that call for forgiveness to resolve. If an enemy develops in your life and you fail to truly forgive your enemy before that lifetime ends, that enemy and you will most likely experience multiple future incarnations together—within the same family unit or in close association.

On a grander scale, forgiveness is the only solution for peace for ongoing conflicts between groups and nations. For instance, the Israeli and Palestinian people both have a right to live upon this Earth. However, their actions toward each other have locked them together in open conflict for many lifetimes.

My spiritual mentor says that both groupings will have to incarnate and live beside each other on this Earth for numerous incarnations more, before they will treat each other with unconditional love. I believe the ultimate lesson to learn is to bring to soul memory, our knowledge of unconditional love.

There is no fear in love, but perfect love casteth out fear: because fear hath torment. He that feareth is not made perfect in love. [1]   1 John 4:18

---

fear apprehension of evil or danger; dread; anxiety   New Websterian

---

7

FEAR AND SOUL MEMORIES

Fear Memories

When we go about our life, freed from the many stresses and struggles that fear-based thoughts and emotions cause, we can live a more balanced, happier life.

Fear as energy is an over-abundance of negative energy. It robs us of our vitality and takes away the good energy we need to stay balanced in our lives. Contrary to the common thought of today, fear does not motivate—it keeps us from a perfect state of balance.

However, our fears can alert us to issues we need to address. It is important to try to uncover the time, place and events that triggered our fears. Whether or not our fears are a result of incidents this lifetime or past lifetimes, it is important to take steps toward changing our reactions to fear-based emotions.

The following is an example of where a past life experience (cause) brought about unexplained fears and anxiety (effect) in a current life experience:

One day, a new client knocked on my front door. When I opened the door, she saw my pet cat, began screaming and was about to run down the street. She was so upset that she vomited outside. I quickly put the cat in another room and went after the client.

As I began to work with her to calm her down, I assured her the cat would not be in the same room with her. I told her there was a door between her and the cat and that I would lock the door. Although she was fearful, she came into the house and hesitantly sat down in a chair across from me.

Once she was calmer, I asked her if she had ever had a negative encounter with a cat. She assured me she had not. I began to sense an event in one of her past lifetimes that caused such a radical reaction on her part. I asked her if her right elbow and left knee hurt. She nodded yes. She related that her doctors had performed many tests, but could not find anything wrong. She felt the doctors thought she was using the pain to get attention, but that was not the case. I then asked if I could tell her what I sensed about her fear of cats. With her permission, I began to tell her what I was seeing:

> Your subconscious mind has stored fears from a past life when you lived in India. You were a male with a small, frail body structure. You had a family and every day you would go to the edge of the jungle and gather herbs and roots to barter for food and necessities for your family.

> Most men in your village also worked in the jungle and were careful not to venture in too far because of the danger of encountering tigers. The tigers had killed and devoured many that did and so it was with great risk that you worked.

> You possessed a keen sense of smell and thought this would alert you to where a tiger(s) had just been. Therefore, you depended upon this sense to warn you when to turn back. Over-harvesting had depleted many of the herbs and roots

you were collecting. You found yourself needing to go farther into the jungle, even though you did not feel safe; you felt you had little choice.

On one particular day, you smelled the tiger and knew you had to take measures to hide from it. You found a dead tree with an opening you could climb inside to hide. You hurried to it and crammed your body up and into the dead tree, holding yourself up with your left knee and right elbow and arm.

The tiger had just eaten but sensed that there was more in the tree; it was not in any hurry.

It was very hot in the dead tree. It seemed as though all the air was absent and a moist mist had replaced it. Your clothing was soaked as was your hair. You soon became numb, almost ready to drop down from the tree and make a run for it. Then it happened.

The tiger's odor got stronger and stronger and it began to make terrible growling noises. It reached up inside the tree, sunk his teeth into your left thigh and jerked you out of the tree.

The tiger tore the bones in your right elbow and left knee out of the sockets and through the flesh. It did not kill you right away. The tiger was not hungry and so it played with your body for a while. You began to go into shock. Not before, however, you felt its whiskers on your face and smelled the breath of the tiger. You could feel the fur against your face and you knew you would surely die.

It was all over quickly. You died from suffocation when the tiger clamped his teeth down into your throat. Horrific terror filled your last moments.

Even though you died quickly, the memory of this event is still within your subconscious mind and the sight of cats releases this fear energy into your consciousness. This is why you are so terrified of cats!

Releasing Fear Memories

After revealing this past life event, I asked her how her elbow felt now. She checked her elbow and was surprised to find the pain was gone. She wanted to know what I had done. I did not answer her question but instead asked her about her knee. She rubbed it a little and said it felt better and again asked me what I had done. I assured her that I had done nothing. She had done it all by herself. She released the unpleasant energy and soul memory that had been so long a part of her. She brought the memory from a past life to a conscious level, acknowledged it and then released it.

This does not mean she will love cats or even like them, she does not have to. However, it does mean she can know and understand the source of her fear. Now, she can tell herself she does not have to react with such fear when she sees a cat. When she watches a cat commercial on TV or sees a cat down the street, she can tell herself now that she has no reason to fear. She knows that her reaction was caused by a past life experience and she has released the energy of the memory.

I have seen this client since the incident at my home. She was much better, even though she still has some fear of cats, she does not react in such an emotional way. She just gives cats their space and chooses not to be around them. She has said that her elbow and knee have not hurt her since she uncovered the painful past life memory.

Unexplained fearful behaviors in young children can also be the result of soul memories. Martha was a former student of mine. After her son, Kit, was born, he often cried and literally went into bouts of panic and screaming for no apparent reason. He always wanted his covers tucked very tight around him at night before he went to sleep or before taking a nap. This seemed to keep him calm.

As these events continued, Martha found she could not predict when he was going to become hysterical. These events occurred whether or not they were at home, shopping, dining out or visiting friends or family. After two and a half years, Martha finally asked for guidance from her dreams. Her dreams revealed to her an important event from a past lifetime, as follows:

> In a previous lifetime, Martha and Kit were part of a Northwestern Indian tribe. In this incarnation, Martha was the mother of Kit and he was still young enough to carry in an Indian child or papoose carrier, a backpack of sorts. Martha would lace the strings snugly and securely in place, which had a calming effect upon him when in a carrier.

The women kept their babies or young children in a carrier while working inside their dwellings or would strap them on their backs while doing chores outside.

Early one morning, an enemy tribe attacked their village. The women and elders grabbed the children and fled quickly into the woods. The men of the tribe stayed behind and fought off the enemy which allowed time for the elders, women and children to scatter in different directions with the hope of escape.

Martha grabbed Kit (in his carrier) and fled into the woods. As she was running, she glanced back, saw small treetops moving in the distance behind her and realized the enemy warriors were in close pursuit.

She stopped suddenly, hid Kit in a thicket and fled in another direction to lead the warriors away from Kit's hiding place. She was unable to outrun the warriors. Unfortunately, she slowed her pace as she neared the edge of a cliff and an enemy warrior overtook her. He picked her up and threw her off the cliff and she fell to her death.

Hostile warriors often attacked Martha's village, so the women had taught the children to stay quiet and still; this was akin to an instinct for survival. No one ever knew where Martha had hidden Kit. He literally starved to death in silence while waiting for his mother to return to him.

When Martha awakened from this dream, she knew what to do to help Kit. Kit's tightly tucked covers must have reminded him of the security of a tightly laced papoose carrier. Martha later noticed that Kit would only panic when he lost sight of her. She now realized what was causing his behavior.

He had brought into this latest incarnation the soul memory of his lonely death in a previous lifetime. He remembered that being silent led to his starvation and death; he was not going to do that again! So, he screamed as loud as he could whenever he lost sight of his mother.

Now that Martha understood the reason for his outbursts, she was able to help him deal with his fear. She would often tell him to stay close to her, that she loved him and that she wanted him with her always. In about two weeks or so, his behavior changed for the better and life for this little boy returned to normal.

It is especially important to know that everything is a learned experience whether in this or a past lifetime. When we look closely at our behaviors and fears, we can observe whether they spring from experiences in this lifetime or not.

We may be afraid of water, yet never had experienced a near-drowning incident. We may be terrified of heights but never have fallen from a high place nor know why. We may be claustrophobic, deadly afraid of closed-in places, and not have had such an experience to cause our fear.

When we meditate, we need to ask when and where we acquired these fears or what is causing us to react. The fears may have originated from a past life or from our present lifetime. We can meditate, search our subconscious and slowly begin to remember the causes.

It is important that we bring these memories to a conscious level, acknowledge the experiences and, then, let them go. Once we see the real cause of our fears, we can release the energy of fear from our soul memories.

Sometimes, we do not see what we have learned from our life experiences, such as patience, tolerance and so forth, until years later. If we would reflect on each experience we have in life, we will find that *we are either learning something or teaching something!*

🕊 *Whosoever hateth his brother is a murderer: and ye know that no murderer hath eternal life abiding in him.* [1]

1 John 3:15

🕊 *Let us not therefore judge one another any more: but judge this rather, that no man put a stumblingblock or an occasion to fall in his brother's way.* [2]

Romans 14:13

8

WHY PEOPLE ARE HOMOSEXUAL

It takes a courageous soul to be reborn into the Earth plane. To choose learning experiences within the norm of society is difficult enough for most souls. However, some souls choose a greater challenge by incarnating into roles outside the norm of society. When we understand the function of these incarnations, we can develop a greater sense of compassion for the souls who make such difficult choices. The intent of the following information channeled from Spirit is to bring forth knowledge of the true nature of homosexuality.

Spirit says this soul grouping is in need of our greater understanding to help lessen the pain and suffering these individuals presently endure and to prevent negative karma by those who dehumanize and persecute homosexuals by thought, word or deed. To my knowledge, no one has yet given the real reason why people are bisexual, heterosexual, homosexual and trans-gendered.

Our earthly experience is one of learning to balance energy. Before incarnating on Earth, our karmic advisors help us plan the learning experiences needed to balance our overall energies. Usually, we do our planning as a member of a soul grouping. We not only plan our earthy experiences in advance, but we decide within our soul grouping which roles each soul will play in each evolutionary experience.   Each soul through its previous incarnations has accumulated a unique understanding of its feminine and masculine energies.

We learn how to balance our feminine and masculine energy through our earthly relationships. Our intimate, loving and enduring relationships help us to balance our energies the most. Within these relationships, we refine our individual energies, balance our human nature and further our spiritual growth.

Once our souls have incarnated back to Earth, sexuality assists in attracting the appropriate people to share our lives. Sexuality is the magnetic force that draws and propels us into a deeper relationship. In addition to being a means of procreation, sex is an exchange of energy and expression of love. Some people are attracted to the same sex or members of the opposite sex. Others are attracted to both females and males.   Since we choose earthly experiences that will lead to the balancing of our energies, we must assume that our sexual orientation is an integral part of this process. Few people, regardless of sexual orientation, understand how our sexual orientation takes shape during our incarnations on Earth.

My spirit mentors say that heterosexuality and homosexuality are the results of the energies that formed from our previous incarnations, that sexuality is just energy, energy, energy! Too much of one kind of energy and not enough of the other creates variations in our human experiences. This is particularly relevant to our sexual energies.

How Past Incarnations Form a Heterosexual Nature

Human life on Earth is essentially about mastering the creative and sustaining qualities of feminine and masculine energy. When we are on the other side ready to incarnate back to the Earth again, it is imperative that we balance our feminine and masculine energies. Generally, this is a two-step process.

One, we balance our feminine and masculine energies by alternating our incarnations or lifetimes as male and female—coming back male, then female, male, then female.

Two, as we alternate gender in each incarnation, we usually establish our most intimate relationships with the opposite sex. This alternating pattern helps to keep our energies balanced. This pattern is neither right or wrong, nor good or bad, just an easier pattern to keep our energies balanced. For very good reasons, souls do not necessarily follow the easiest pattern, as we shall see!

How Past Incarnations Form a Homosexual Nature

Remember, we have free will—even while we are in the nonphysical realms. We have karmic advisors, but the final decision is ours. When a soul chooses to come back again and again as the same sex, then there is an over-abundance of that energy and soul memory. A soul will tend to express itself in much the same way it had in the previous incarnations.

Let us consider a homosexual male with an over-abundance of feminine energy. If a soul had previously incarnated many lifetimes as a female without alternating genders, he, as a male in this lifetime, would have an over-abundance of feminine energy and soul memories. In addition, he would be just as attracted to men in this lifetime as he had been in the previous lifetimes when he had incarnated as a female.

Again, gay men's attraction for males will be quite natural to them; this attraction is *their soul memory of a strong energy pattern reinforced over many lifetimes.* Homosexuality is neither right or wrong, nor good or bad, just the effect of the energy and soul memory from past incarnations.

The Ultimate Conscientious Objectors

Society's negative attitudes and actions toward this grouping can make incarnations of homosexuals extremely challenging. It is with these thoughts in mind that I sought answers from my spiritual mentors. If repeated female incarnations lead to an over-abundance of feminine energy and a challenging male incarnation, why would a soul make such a choice?

According to my spiritual mentors, ever since the spirit of man entered a physical body, the male of the species has had to kill. If souls came to Earth as males, they had to kill in wars because wars were ongoing, war after war after war. Then, my spiritual guides related, *"Now remember, it is against the nature of the Spirit to kill!"*

I had never considered this aspect of soul choice. Men are homosexual because they did not want to come to Earth as males during times of war and instead, they chose many consecutive lifetimes as females.

According to my spiritual guides, the vast majority of gay men on Earth today chose not to kill in their previous incarnations on Earth. They made those decisions knowing that they would eventually suffer the consequences of inequitable treatment, as homosexuals, in later incarnations. This was a decision made not just by individuals, but also by an enormous, self-select soul grouping, as outlined below:

Many, many lifetimes ago, there was a major agreement on the other side, a spiritual revolution and resolve by millions of souls, that in their evolutionary path toward perfection through their incarnations on Earth, THEY WOULD NOT KILL. In this resolve of non-violence and compassion for all souls, they in effect, knowingly sacrificed themselves lifetime after lifetime by choosing a more difficult evolutionary journey through the Earth plane.

By this decision, millions of souls withdrew their energies permanently from the field of violence on Earth. The magnitude of violence and killing during the wars on Earth would have been much greater had these souls failed to make this resolve of non-violence and compassion. It was their freewill choice to incarnate as females in lifetime after lifetime in order not to kill their fellow human beings.

When these same souls incarnate on Earth, they incarnate as homosexual males. As homosexual males, they often experience society's harsh, negative reaction to their sexuality. Experiencing this is not the result of any negative personal karma, but is the direct consequences of their soul choice not to kill in their many previous lifetimes.

The Wounding of the Spirit

When a person kills another human, the act of killing not only kills the other person but also wounds the Spirit of the person that did the killing. It is against the nature of the Spirit, our Spirit, to kill.

For example, soldiers have often joined the military out of a true sense of patriotism to defend their country. Many have entered the military at a young age before they had enough experience to formulate their own value system. When soldiers kill someone in defense of their country, they do what they are trained and ordered to do.

However, each time they kill, it wounds more and more of their own Spirit. In time as the shock of killing accumulates within, they may elect to transfer to another branch of service or position themselves within military activities that will not require them to kill.

When soldiers kill, the shock of that killing stays with them. This affects their life long after the killing took place. It is for this reason that every soldier who kills should have ongoing counseling.

Approximately forty percent of the soldiers who kill will have problems thereafter that strongly and sometimes tragically affect their lives. The wounding of their Spirit causes disturbing dreams, ongoing flashbacks of the killing and results in extreme emotional / mental stress. My guides say that this wounding of the Spirit is one of the primary causes of Post-traumatic Stress Disorder (PTSD).

The wounding of their Spirit adversely affects the quality of their relationships with family, friends and coworkers. PTSD pushes some soldiers to leave a military career, avoid others and eventually they may go into total seclusion.

Certain activities will cause flashbacks of previous killing and the soldiers often use drugs and alcohol as coping mechanisms. Their alcohol and drug use is an attempt to dull the senses to the wounding of their own Spirit and to forget the killing of other human beings.

With each lifetime, it becomes more unbearable to kill as the compassion grows within the consciousness of their soul. This is one reason why, my guides say, people become conscientious objectors, choose not to kill or go to war. They cannot tolerate the killing any more. My heart goes out to the soldiers because of the suffering they will endure.

Not only is it against the nature of the Spirit to kill but also to torture any life form. Eventually, many will refuse to be involved in killing animals as a food source and will become vegetarians and gravitate toward working for organizations that protect animal life.

The Peacemakers

I further asked my spiritual mentor, if men are homosexual because they did not want to kill, does this mean that lesbians wanted to kill in their previous incarnations? My mentor replied this was not the case. Since there were wars and killings, there had to be peacemakers and mediators.

There were a large number of souls, who volunteered to come back as males for consecutive lifetimes and voice their concerns, so they could help bring about peace. In those days, women had no voice. Therefore, no woman could pass the peace pipe, talk peace at the table or sign a treaty.

That made sense to me but I wondered about us so called "straight ones." My spiritual mentor said, "Maybe you have been lucky. However, you will have your time to bring about peace, wait and see."

My granddaughter and her husband went to Washington D.C. with a group to march in a peace rally that aired on CSPAN TV. I watched it from the very beginning. There was a lot of music and many people talking about peace. The energy was very high there, as it always is, when peace is in the thoughts of a very large number of people. I was very proud of the people who had the courage to speak out and march for peace.

According to my spiritual guides, the majority of the women on the platform at the peace rally were lesbians. These souls kept coming back as men in previous lifetimes so they could help stop the killing, and are still trying to stop it. They are not in male bodies this lifetime, because women have gained a greater voice, the right to vote, be educated and work in fields previously dominated by men. Countries are now even drafting women for military service. However, females / lesbians are still trying to get their foot in the door, so to speak, to stop the wars and the killing.

I asked my spiritual guides, if the killing on the planet would stop and what will happen with homosexual incarnations if the killing on Earth does stop? Spirit said the killing will stop, but not for many, many lifetimes and after numerous calamities and misfortunes. Eventually, Jesus will walk the Earth with humankind and peace will reign. We will all be as brothers and sisters around the world. Since peace will prevail, there will be no need to get the energies out of balance.

Reincarnation will still exist as we have not yet perfected our souls and learned all the lessons we need to learn. Some of us will come back as teachers and some to perfect our nature. We will eventually choose to alternate lifetimes as male then female, male then female until we balance our feminine and masculine energy. There will be no more homosexual expressions in the human experience and homosexuality will cease to exist.

Remember, homosexuality is neither right nor wrong, or good or bad. It is a case of "cause and effect." The "cause" is just an over-abundance of either masculine or feminine energy. The "effect" is women attracted to women or men attracted to men. This over-abundance of feminine or masculine energy manifests from their past incarnations.

Cause and Effect Energy Variations

Until the perfection of our will with God's, almost all souls are born with varying degrees of an over-abundance or under-abundance of feminine or masculine energy. People do not have to be homosexual to have this energy affect aspects of their personality and life. Each time a soul chooses not to have the energy balanced by alternating male and female lifetimes, he or she will have a "cause–effect" with the energy on a gender / sexual basis. As the number of repetitive, same gender incarnations increase, the over-abundance of energy and soul memory increases.

The following is a brief, simplified overview of soul expressions starting at an over-abundance of energy at the maximum and decreasing in over-abundance to the minimum expression (from the trans-gendered to the cross-dresser):

MALES BORN WITH AN OVER-ABUNDANCE OF FEMININE ENERGY:

AN OVER-ABUNDANCE OF ENERGY AT THE MAXIMUM WOULD BRING INTO THE EARTH PLANE MALES WHO ARE TRANS-GENDERED OR WILL BE TRANS-GENDERED AND EVENTUALLY HAVE REASSIGNMENT SURGERY.

From the beginning, they wanted to be the opposite sex and always wanted to be a girl when they were born a boy. They felt like a girl and never felt like a little boy. As they grew older, they wanted to dress in women's clothing, walk, talk and act effeminate. They become depressed and tormented by this internally sometimes to the point of suicide.

The ones that are lucky will have access to appropriate psychologists and other mental health professionals and will receive counseling. If they choose a competent counselor, they will be encouraged to start hormone treatments and, eventually, reassignment surgery.

Once the change is complete, the males who have trans-gendered into female bodies feel like they have come home. They usually say, "Oh, thank you, thank you God. Now, I am who I really was all along. I did not look like a woman until now. But I always felt like a woman." They had tuned into their excess feminine energy and soul memory of having come to the Earth so many times as a female. The feminine energy is so strong that even though they are in a male body, they feel like a female. That is why they want to dress like a female and long to be a woman.

When they finally became a female from the reassignment surgery, they felt at peace. They felt like at last they were in the body, they should have been in all along. Even though they have gone through the reassignment process, they have taken the initial steps to rebalance their energy by incarnating in a male body.

DECREASING DOWN TO THE NEXT LEVEL OF AN OVER-ABUNDANCE OF FEMININE ENERGY WILL BE MALES THAT ARE USUALLY FLAMBOYANT, GAY AND WHO DRESS VERY FLAMBOYANTLY IN WOMEN'S ATTIRE .

They do not desire so much to be female but like the role-playing as a female. They like to be in women's clothing. They will still be attracted to men and want to be with men in a gay life style. The energy has not driven them to want to change their sex; they just act out the energy in a flamboyant way.

NEXT, WE GO DOWN ANOTHER LEVEL, WHICH IS STILL AN OVER-ABUNDANCE OF FEMININE ENERGY NOT AS STRONG AS THE TRANS-GENDERED OR THE FLAMBOYANT GAY.

They will still be gay, very effeminate and would maybe like to dress up once and awhile but not in a real flamboyant manner.

DOWN ANOTHER LEVEL, WE HAVE THE HOMOSEXUAL MALES WHO ARE THE STRAIGHT GAY GUYS.

They live a gay lifestyle and usually have one partner.

THEN, WE HAVE THE LATENT HOMOSEXUALS.

Homosexuality remains dormant within them. They are still gay, but they do not act on it, maybe due to a fear of their family or society's reaction to homosexuality. They will have effeminate characteristics and usually are very loving and sensitive individuals, but not really fulfilled within themselves. Although they find relationships with women not very fulfilling, they will usually marry the opposite gender. They will be unfulfilled because they are not acting on what is truly inside their hearts.

NEXT, WE HAVE TRANSVESTITES WHO DRESS IN WOMAN'S CLOTHES AND USUALLY GO OUT IN PUBLIC IN WOMEN'S CLOTHING.

They do not have a desire to be trans-gendered or a flamboyant gay or anything like that. They are just transvestites and most are not gay.

FINALLY, WE HAVE MEN WHO JUST LIKE TO DRESS UP—THE CROSS-DRESSER, BUT THEY USUALLY ARE NOT GAY.

The feminine energy is just a tad over-abundant. They like the feel of women's clothing, like silk stockings and lingerie. They will usually have a closet full of women's clothing. I know a man with three closets full and he dresses at home only. Usually, no one knows about it, and this part of his life takes place in the privacy of his own home.

FEMALES BORN WITH AN OVER-ABUNDANCE OF MASCULINE ENERGY:

FEMALES WITH AN OVER-ABUNDANCE OF MASCULINE ENERGY AT THE MAXIMUM WOULD BRING INTO THE EARTH PLANE INDIVIDUALS WHO ARE TRANS-GENDERED OR WILL BE TRANS-GENDERED AND EVENTUALLY HAVE REASSIGNMENT SURGERY.

The characteristics are like the trans-gendered males with an over-abundance of feminine energy as mentioned above, but the gender roles are reversed.

THE NEXT EXPRESSION WITH AN OVER-ABUNDANCE OF MASCULINE ENERGY IS THE REMAINDER OF THE HOMOSEXUAL WOMEN.

Homosexual females with an over-abundance of masculine energy generally do not experience the wide variations in expressions as homosexual males experience with an over-abundance of feminine energy.

[*My dear readers, I sincerely hope in my attempts to bring understanding in the generalizations made above (as to the importance of energy and soul memories and the resulting expressions) that I have not offended anyone.*]

There are women saying that they are lesbians when they are just bisexual. Bisexuals tend to like being with both sexes. That is a choice they make and it is not anything they brought into this Earth. Making such a choice is not a result of karma nor does it create negative karma. There is not an over-abundance of any energy compelling them to be with both sexes. It is just their freewill choice.

Regarding the different energy expressions of males and females listed above, not all expressions are homosexual. According to Spirit, homosexuals make up approximately thirty percent of the world's current population. My spiritual mentors emphasize that homosexuality with consenting adults is neither good or bad, nor right or wrong. *Homosexuality is not a religious, psychiatric or psychological issue—it is just a matter of energy and soul memories.*

My spiritual mentors tell me that God does not judge us. We judge ourselves when we make the transition to the spirit world after our physical death. If it is a perverted thought in the mind, it is a perverted act whether we are bisexual, heterosexual, homosexual, or trans-gendered. God loves each and everyone just the same. God never gives up on us. Being a homosexual is never an issue because when we die, we can see that it is just a matter of an over-abundance of energy and soul memories.

If there is an over-abundance of the feminine energy with male incarnations, they will come back as homosexual males. If there is an over-abundance of masculine energy with female incarnations, they will come back as homosexual females. It is that simple. People incarnate with their energy and soul memories and cannot change being homosexual if they wanted to. It will take many lifetimes to balance the energy.

Consider a gay man. He will have to keep coming back as a male until the energy is balanced. Then, he can afford to be female only a few times lest he create an over-abundance of energy again. We control and balance our sexual energies by our choices of whether to be male or female in our incarnations.

Since Earth is a schoolhouse for learning, our every action is one of freewill choice. The main reason God created different cultures, nationalities, races and religions was so humankind could learn lessons and unconditional love through freewill choice.

As these particular groupings of souls struggle through difficult incarnations, it is important to remember that they are sparks of the divine and, as such, are inherently spiritual beings. *All people are a part of the divine—they just take different paths on their evolutionary journey back to the source.*

PART TWO

9

RECEIVING GUIDANCE THROUGH DREAMS
James Daniels, Contributing Author

10

ACCESSING INFORMATION THROUGH DOWSING
James Daniels, Contributing Author

11

LOOK UP!
(CONCLUDING VISION AND PRAYER)
Nan Moore, Author

REFLECTIONS and ADDENDUM
Nan Moore, Author

And it shall come to pass afterward, that I will pour out my spirit upon all flesh; and your sons and your daughters shall prophesy, your old men shall dream dreams, your young men shall see visions: And also upon the servants and upon the handmaids in those days I pour out my spirit. [1]

Joel 2:28-29

9

RECEIVING GUIDANCE THROUGH DREAMS

by James Daniels, contributing author

I first met the author, Nan Moore, when she gave me a psychic reading at her home in 1980. During the reading, she impressed me with the clarity of her psychic gifts and the ease by which the information flowed through her. She nailed events in my past, summarized my current activities and revealed decisions I would likely make in the future. She also knew what I was thinking about my reading while simultaneously giving me the reading! I was mesmerized, as the magnitude of her gifts swirled within my head.

Suddenly in my mind's eye, I saw psychic, Nan Moore, in a duel with the metaphysical non-believers of the world. With her pistols cocked and loaded with an arsenal of psychic bullets, it was no contest. She was the real McCoy. The non-believers didn't stand a chance!

A somewhat serious voice brought me out of my daydreaming as Nan asked, "Jim, do you have any questions about your reading?"

After the reading ended, I noticed that the room looked like a classroom where individuals would sit around a large table. I asked Nan if she taught classes and she replied that she did offer classes to the public. Because of my inquiry, a friend of mine and I started attending her meditation and psychic development classes.

In class, she stressed the use of meditation as a foundation for attunement and for the development of psychic gifts. She encouraged her students to start with learning only one or two methods of receiving psychic information. She introduced a number of different methods, but the method we mostly used in class was psychometry.

Once the classes got underway, it did not take long for me to realize that I was about as psychic as a goat. Now a goat is smart in many ways and often downright charming, but psychic, it is not.

Therefore, as this goat continued to sit in class, it noticed that its peers were, slowly but surely, starting to receive bits of psychic information as they practiced their psychometry from week to week. In each successive class, Nan would put different objects in a covered bowl and each of us would reach in and pull out an object with which to practice psychometry.

The way it worked was to hold an object we had selected and then give our impressions of the owner of the object—*aloud*, so all there would know how psychically deficient this goat really was. Smile. Especially Nan, who could probably recount my regressed lineage back to Methuselah's personal goatherd while watching TV and baking an apple pie.

About three weeks into the class, I took hold of my selected object and began to mumble, "Uh, it is cold, long, lightweight, may be plastic." Even my peers, seemed to groan inwardly, as they began to mentally size up my lack of progress.

In the fourth week of classes, with eyes tightly closed I reached into the covered bowl and pulled out what was obviously a quarter. At least this time, I would be able to describe in detail the object in my hand. Even if one had fingers as callused as a rhino's foot, he or she could tell it was George Washington's face embossed on its surface. I was very proud of myself as I rubbed my fingers around the sharp serrations on the outside edge of that quarter and proudly announced that it was a new quarter. That is, until I opened my eyes and saw how the rest of the class members were looking at me with pity.

However, after about seven or eight weeks of classes, something surprising did happen, not in class but at home, while asleep in my bed. No longer was I viewing dull, lifeless black, gray and white scenery in my dreams, as a panorama of dreams now appeared in brilliant hues and tints of color.

I may be as psychic as a goat but even a goat can dream in living color. Now, let's get serious!

Rediscovering the Importance of Dreams

The Ancients recognized dreams as an invaluable source of guidance and information. The dreams and visions in the Bible are evidence of this truth. If we were to remove all the hundreds of dreams and visions from the Bible, very little of the true essence of the Bible would remain and much of God's early guidance *transmitted through dreams and visions* to humankind would be lost forever.

Yes, the religious leaders today recite the few more commonly known dreams such as the ones of Daniel that enabled him to interpret successfully the dreams of the king and elevate himself to a high position in the kingdom. Also, the dreams of Joseph that so irked his eleven other brothers that they devised a plot to kill him and in which he eventually triumphed over all they did to him. This is about where, nowadays, the focus on dreams in most churches ends.

It is as if the value of dreams as guidance was a one-era phenomena, meant only for the people of that biblical time and place. Of course, there are many other (non-biblical) historical accounts from Egyptian, Tibetan and Grecian cultures and others, which attest to the value of dreams as guidance.

Oddly enough, what has sparked a renewed interest in the study of dreams in the last century is the scientific research coming from dream labs within our universities. That same dream research has documented the fact that we all dream whether or not we recall our dreams and that dreaming is crucial to our health and wellbeing.

Numerous studies revealed that if someone interrupts our dreaming each time we start to dream, we would begin to disintegrate mentally and physically in about one to three days. I inadvertently discovered this fact when first experimenting with my own dream states (which I write about later on in this chapter). So dreaming is essential for human life to exist, regardless of our cultural and religious beliefs.

You can tell when a person is dreaming. You really do not require a fancy dream laboratory—you already have one, your bed! First, you must act as if you are already asleep. Second, when it is obvious that your mate is asleep, roll over on your side and watch your mate's closed eyelids. When your mate's eyes start to dart back and forth and up and down rapidly, that mate is dreaming.

If you are sleeping with a *non-believer*, a mate who denies the existence of dreams, just wake her or him up while they are having those little rapid-eye movements. That mate's dream recall, at that point, will be vivid. Presto, you have created your own *dream believer*, right in your very own dream lab. In a similar fashion, I successfully conducted my own dream experiments, that is, until my first wife divorced me! Smile.

Everyone is truly psychic and everyone dreams while asleep. As you begin to work with your dreams, you will be utterly amazed at the many possibilities that will emerge and the quality of the information that you can receive through your dreams.

Dreams have sparked many great works and discoveries by artists, inventors, musicians, scientists, writers and the like. They somehow learned to receive guidance through their dreams and knew how to recall that information upon awakening.

Innovative and astute people often pay close attention to information from their dreams and the reveries that occur at the edge of sleep. Reveries are brief dream-like images that occur just before going to sleep and just before awakening. One such person was the famous inventor, Thomas Edison who used his dreams, especially reveries, to obtain information to get invention ideas and help with the implementation of projects.

While visiting Greenfield Village in Dearborn, Michigan, a tour guide at Edison's Menlo Park Laboratory told me that Thomas Edison would often do experiments to test the best ways to recall the contents of his dreams. Edison would take short naps to get information, mostly about his inventions. He experimented with taking naps while sitting in a chair. He would hold a metal ball in each hand as he held his arms straight down by the sides of his chair. As he entered the edge of sleep, he received dream information just before his body would enter a deeper level of relaxing sleep.

Then, as he drifted into sleep, the muscles in his hands relaxed allowing the metal balls to drop out of his hands and fall into metal pans that he had set on the floor directly beneath each hand. The noise from this improvised timing-mechanism would awaken him right at the end of the dream reverie resulting in better dream recall. Now, isn't that a hoot!

How Dreams Became Important to Me

The very first metaphysical book I read, was titled *Edgar Cayce: The Sleeping Prophet*, by Jess Stearn. My reaction to the book was one of disbelief. With no prior exposure to metaphysical literature, it was inconceivable to me that a person could get such detailed information from a higher consciousness. Even more incredible, that the guidance and help received was seemingly limitless.

I decided to test and see if I could receive information from my own dreams and subconscious. I was doubtful about my prospects since I rarely remembered my dreams and knew so little about dreams.

Most dream researchers emphasize the importance of pre-sleep suggestions to insure a better recall of dreams. Shortly before falling asleep, they recommend saying a pre-sleep suggestion such as the following, "I will remember my dreams after I have awakened in the morning." They also suggest you place a pen and note pad or recorder near your bed to record your dreams upon awakening. Don't do anything until you have remembered and recorded the previous night's dreams. If you start the day's activities without recording your dreams first, the memory of the dreams will fade and you will be less likely to recall the dreams later on in the day.

With my first attempt, I had not read the pre-sleep suggestions carefully enough and, as a result, left out an essential part of the pre-sleep suggestion. I had suggested, "I will awaken after each dream and remember the dream after I have dreamt it. The result was I would wake up at the end of each and every dream throughout the night and write down my dreams.

In no time, I was remembering five or six dreams per night. Although amazed by my success, after three nights I was exhausted! I was not getting enough sleep, even though my less than perfect pre-sleep suggestions produced excellent dream recall. I knew something was wrong. Therefore, I re-read examples of pre-sleep suggestions and amended my suggestion to say, "I will remember my dreams *after I have awakened in the morning*." I then got it right and successfully remembered my dreams, after a full night's worth of uninterrupted sleep!

Since the early days of my youth, I have had in the neighborhood of two hundred recurring nightmares because of severe throat and bronchial infections with temperatures reaching well over 101 degrees. Upon awakening from these nightmares, I would remember seeing an ongoing invasion of mean, little critters. They were multiplying, ☹ ☹ ☹ ☹ ☹ ☹ ☹ ☹ ☹ ☹ ☹ overwhelming and killing a much smaller number of tiny white critters ☺ ☺ ☺ ☺ and my life was in jeopardy.

At that time, I did not consider nightmares as dreams and I did not even know why I was having the nightmares. Obviously, I did not have one whit of intuition then, because the meanings of those nightmares seem so obvious to me now. What I was seeing was the throat and bronchial infection systematically overcoming my body's defenses to protect it.

After I learned how to interpret my dreams (when the infections raised my body temperature way above 101 degrees), I realized how serious my illness was and that I needed more than just medical intervention—thankfully, I was paying close enough attention to my dreams to receive input about the actual cause of my illness.

As a result of testing Cayce's dream guidance, my life would never be the same again. His work revealed to me the vastness of our human potential and the usefulness of our dreams. Even though some dreams appear to us as nightmares and grab our attention—our dreams do not harm us but actually help guide us safely through our lives.

Building a New Life

After eight years of marriage to my first wife and in the midst of a divorce, I was depressed and often absent from work. The life I had known with my spouse and all of our plans were suddenly over. I felt lost, miserable and did not know what to do next.

One night before sleep, I asked for guidance through my dream state. I asked for the highest and best source to give me input about what I should do with my life. I awakened about 5:00 a.m. one morning, after having the following dream:

I was sitting, front and center, in a large auditorium. I was the only person there because the presentation was for me. On the elevated stage directly in front of me were seated three men. They were Albert Schweitzer, Aleksandr Solzhenitsyn and Albert Einstein. Their demeanor was serious.

Then, Albert Einstein stood up, took hold of the odd-looking chair he had been sitting in and said, "Jim, look carefully at this chair. I made every part of this chair to fit me. When I sit in it, it fits me perfectly and does not cut off the circulation in my legs." (In the dream the chair looked like a homemade chair someone might place on the front porch of an old log cabin).

Finally he said, "Jim, make your own chair and make every part of it to fit you!" After he said that, Schweitzer and Solzhenitsyn nodded their heads in agreement with him.

Essentially, these great souls were telling me to make a life that would fit my own understanding and needs, not someone else's.

Shortly after having this dream, my marriage ended and I was suddenly on my own. This dream proved prophetic, as I began to reshape my life to fit my own understanding and needs. Not too long after that, I took a leave of absence from my job, moved out of state and enrolled in college.

I had been out of high school for nine years and was concerned I might flunk out of college. I studied hard, did not date and as a result made very good grades. At the beginning of the second year of college, I decided that I would start dating but I was unsure that I could date and still maintain a high grade point average.

There was a sophomore student (let us call him Allen), who had already taken all the sophomore classes that I would be taking. While talking with him at length in my dorm room, I soon realized that he had an extra-sensory gift, a photographic memory!

As he continued to talk, I got lost in thought. I was thinking about his ability to recall in minute detail all that he had heard, seen or read, when a truly novel and exciting plan emerged from my small, freshman brain. It suddenly occurred to me that this *sophomore memory genius* was the key to my plan to "date more and study less." I immediately asked Allen to give me a verbal analysis and study plan of all classes and professors (as I grabbed a yellow note pad and pen to write it all down).

Allen proceeded to give me the most detailed precise study plan that I could have ever imagined possible. With Allen's study plan, I figured that I could reduce my study time by thirty percent during my sophomore year, make just as good grades and have plenty of time for dating. I could almost hear the Hallelujah chorus singing in the background!

Allen's gift provided a breakthrough in my dating dilemma. My success with this endeavor renewed my interest in developing my own abilities, particularly, in using dreams as guidance.

Using Dreams to Find a Date or Mate

While thinking about this dating matter, I got the idea to do a pre-sleep suggestion in which I would ask for the identity of the "best woman at the college" for me. Early the next morning, I recalled the following dream:

> I was standing in the middle of a vast desert. There was only sand as far as the eye could see in every direction. A small speck of something appeared on the distant horizon. I continued to watch this tiny speck as it grew larger and soon I could see that someone was riding a camel towards me. As the rider and camel got closer, I could see that the rider was a beautiful young woman.
>
> The camel stopped near me, dropped down onto its knees and the woman swiftly slid off the animal to the ground. Then, she walked over, stood in front of me with a beautiful

smile and said, "My name is Ellen (of course, not her real name)."

I actually woke myself up from the dream, by loudly exclaiming to myself, *"I have seen this woman on campus! My God, this dream stuff is fantastic!"* I later met her and struck up a conversation with her. She turned out to be a very nice lady and we did date but not for long. I initially thought I had received the information that I really wanted, but something kept bothering me about that dream. After receiving some inner promptings, I further researched the symbols contained in my dream and soon discovered what was wrong.

I realized I should have paid closer attention to how the answer to my dream request was delivered in the dream. The woman in the dream came out of the desert riding a camel towards me. I had limited my dream request to the best woman for me at a small college (the desert where few people live). My dream request answer was delivered to me on a camel (a camel is considered a dumb animal). What was dumb was my dream request of limiting the best woman for me to the population of a small college campus.

Nan Moore had said in Chapter 2, when wording our prayers that we should not ask for a specific thing. Instead, we should ask for what we are destined to have.

I believe this applies to our dream requests as well. Had I asked, "Who is the person I am destined to be with (instead of who is the best woman at this college for me)?" Then, *I would have asked the best possible question and received the best possible answer.*

(Over time since my college days, I have compiled some helpful guidance in structuring pre-sleep suggestions for my own personal use. I have placed these at the end of this chapter, for those of you who would like a starting point by which to seek your own guidance from your dreams.)

After figuring out the desert dream, I amended my pre-sleep suggestion and asked for the best woman in the world for me. Then, I had the following dream:

> I saw before me a lady with short, dark brown hair and beside her was a little, red headed girl. They both had their faces veiled with their facial features obscured.

Over the next fifteen years, I would have the same recurring dream. In each dream, their faces remained veiled.

While working at a community college, someone told me that the husband of a math instructor had suddenly died of a heart attack. That following night I had the same recurring dream of the veiled lady with a little girl, but in this dream both their faces were unveiled—visible and distinct. The lady in my dreams was Linda, the math instructor (whose husband had died suddenly) and the little redheaded girl turned out to be her younger daughter.

As you can imagine, it is difficult to judge the appropriate time to approach a woman after her spouse of nineteen years had died. Therefore, I did not express an interest for quite some time after that.

Then, a nursing instructor at the college told me that she had abruptly wakened after a dream she had and she remembered that she was very upset with me. I asked her why she was upset with me in the dream. She said the only thing she could remember was that she kept shouting at me repeatedly in the dream saying, "Now is the time that Linda will need you the most!" She then told me she had no idea what the dream meant.

After having the same recurring dream for fifteen years, with the face of my intended life companion *veiled* and in a more recent dream with the face of my destined mate *unveiled, I certainly knew then what the significance of the nursing instructor's dream was!*

Heeding Warning Dreams and Changing the Future

One of the most important aspects of dreams is their potential to help us shape the future. I found this to be true in my own life. When I got off track in my life, dreams warned me of possible dangers and helped redirect my course towards a more desirable outcome and future.

After graduating from college, I was hired by a corporation as an administrator and responsible for the health and safety of all its employees. The nature of the company's business made it one of the most hazardous in the industry. The company further charged me with creating, staffing and operating an entirely new department. It was a very challenging and stressful undertaking.

A mystery illness took a heavy toll on my health soon after I started work there. I would often end up in the emergency room of the local hospital on weekends seeking treatment.

Seeing no improvement in my condition, the hospital eventually referred me to a medical specialist to check for possible allergies. After pricking the skin on my back and testing for a variety of allergens, the specialist told me that I was allergic to a host of different things and that I needed to give myself two injections of allergy medicine twice a day, every day. In short order, I was able to work without feeling sick and thought all was well. Yet, I had the following nightmare:

I saw myself dead, face down in the dirt with no shirt on
and I had about 50 hypodermic needles sticking in my back.
They were identical to the hypodermic needles I had been
using to give myself allergy shots.

I awakened from the dream quite concerned. After much worry
and consideration, I decided to reduce my injections by half, thinking
that I was taking too many shots and that was why I was dead, face
down in the dirt in the dream. The following day I gave myself only
one injection of allergy medicine, twice per day. That same night I
woke up after having yet another nightmare:

Like the first dream, I was dead, face down in the dirt but
this time, I only had about half the number of needles in my
back as I did in the first dream!

After this dream, I was very concerned about continuing to take
any more shots but I had to be healthy enough to work. A large
number of people were depending on me. I decided to ask for dream
advice before going to sleep the following night. My pre-sleep question
was, "What should I do about my health because I need to be healthy
and ALIVE in order to work?" This time all I remembered after
awakening from my next dream was:

I was watching someone pour milk from a glass pitcher into
a tall, clear drinking glass.

I really didn't like drinking milk but I loved cheese, Italian food
with cheese and ice cream. This dream was confusing to me. Before
going to sleep the next night, I asked that *I receive information in my*

dreams in such a way that I would understand the full meaning of my dream. Then, I dreamt the following:

> Again, I was watching someone pour milk from a glass pitcher into a tall, clear drinking glass and then I heard a voice say, "Stop consuming milk products and your health problems will go away."

As a result of this dream, I stopped eating milk products, ceased my allergy injections and seldom have throat, bronchial, and fever issues since. My dreams revealed to me the actual cause of my illnesses; that I was lactose intolerant. This condition had made my body sensitive to allergens such as dust, pollen and a number of other things.

Another example of a serious dream warning occurred shortly after *I had literally married the woman of my dreams* (Linda of the veiled ladies' dream). When Jessica, the veiled little redheaded dream girl (now my stepdaughter) was about two and a half years old, I had the following warning dream:

> The door to the basement stairs was open; I saw little Jessica start down the stairs. After about two steps she fell, rolled under the wooden handrail and off the staircase and tumbled headfirst toward the concrete basement floor below. The weight of her body pushed her head and neck sideways as she hit the floor. The fall had broken her neck and I realized she was not breathing and that the fall had proved fatal.

I woke up right after the dream and told my wife. After much discussion, we felt we needed to put a safety net along the staircase, immediately. Because of the serious nature of the dream, we didn't want to take any chances. Therefore, I got dressed, went to the barn, got some metal hardware screen and stapled it to the handrail and staircase the entire distance down the staircase. I then went back to sleep.

About a month later as I came into the house, I saw little Jessica start down that same staircase. Before I could stop her, she fell, rolled into the wire screen along the hand rail (at the exact same place as in my dream), was deflected back onto the padded staircase and slid down the staircase unharmed. We were so thankful for the guidance we received in this particular warning dream. That little red headed girl in my dreams, my stepdaughter, is now a young adult and attending college.

Enriching Your Life

There are many kinds of dreams. Dreams can help you with health issues, job and business decision-making, interpersonal relationships, generating new ideas and much more. Dreams often serve as a springboard to higher states of consciousness such as astral projection, lucid dreaming, prophetic dreams and visions.

When you are in the dream state, you can see the future, receive guidance and explore other dimensions. Acting as an independent researcher on your own, you might even discover an unknown use of dreams to help others or discover a psychic ability within that awaits your activation and development.

When the author, Nan Moore, asked me to contribute a chapter or two to this book, I was happy to do so. I was especially eager to share with our readers the many ways I have received guidance from my own dreams and demonstrate how dreams have enriched my life and the lives of others.

You can do as I have done and even more. You are already dreaming. All that you have to do is consciously work with the dreaming process and pay particular attention to what your dreams are trying to reveal to you. If you do this, I am confident that you will begin to reap the rewards of an endless flow of invaluable information and guidance.

PRE-SLEEP SUGGESTIONS

- Ask that the highest and best possible information be given in your dreams from your highest self and through what you consider your highest spiritual source, such as Buddha, Christ, Krishna, Mohammed, the Great Spirit or God. The intent here is to ask for the most appropriate information for you and to invoke spiritual guidance and protection.

- Clearly state the problem, project or idea in which you need help.

- Then say, I ask that the dream information to be given will be the best for all concerned. Why do this? Because this affirmation will prevent you from inadvertently doing harm to yourself or anyone else with the information that you are going to receive. In addition, this will prevent you from selling yourself short or someone else with a less than perfectly constructed dream request.

- Then say, I will remember my dreams after I awaken in the morning" and then, go to sleep.

No matter what dream information you receive, you should always ask this question: Is the dream advice or your interpretation of this dream consistent with your values? If not, forget the dream. Do not use the dream information!

> 🕊 *Moreover the word of the Lord came unto me, saying, Jeremiah, what seest thou? And I said, I see a rod of an almond tree. Then said the Lord unto me, Thou hast well seen: for I will hasten my word to perform it.* [1]
>
> Jeremiah 1:11-12

10

ACCESSING INFORMATION THROUGH DOWSING

by James Daniels, contributing author

The ancient art of divining is a practice known as dowsing in America. Doodlebugging, muscle testing, radiesthesia and water witching are other names for dowsing both here and abroad.

Dowsing by any name is the process of seeking information that exists beyond the ability of our five physical senses to perceive it. Dowsing somehow allows a dowser temporarily to disassociate from perceived feelings, opinions or biases of the mind to receive new input, previously unknown to that dowser.

If you ask a thousand dowsers how dowsing actually works, each would most likely give you a different answer. If you were to ask author and psychic, Nan Moore, how dowsing works, she will tell you that "a non-physical helper, such as an angel or guide, intercedes when someone dowses and directs the dowsing device (forked stick, pendulum, rods, etc.) to where water, precious stones, minerals, oil and the like are located."

Skeptics, novices, and seasoned dowsers alike get all wrapped up in debates as to how dowsing actually works or doesn't work. However, what convinces me that dowsing works is the quality and quantity of information that is obtainable through the use of dowsing.

In the past, dowsers used a forked branch of a peach, willow or witch-hazel tree to find underground veins of potable water. This was a common practice in the farming or country areas in America. The dowsers held a forked branch in their hands as they walked over the land until which time the other end of the forked branch dipped sharply down or upward. When this happened, it was purported that the dowsers knew by experience that they had located a good place to dig a well.

Dowsing has long been a widespread practice to locate a good source of water. Dowsing has had many other practical applications as well.

Today, plumbers or excavators often use dowsing to indicate the exact location of underground electrical lines, phone cables and gas and water pipes, instead of digging blindly into the ground. Dowsing before digging or drilling underground has the potential to prevent costly and time-consuming repairs.

Capturing My Attention

A friend, a county judge, once asked me to help him build a fence between the front of his house and the state highway. He knew that this new fence would cross a buried water line on his property. Even though the county water department had previously marked the location of the water line for him, he was concerned that the hydraulic post-driver would rupture the county water line when we pounded the wooden fence posts into the ground.

After pondering this, he suddenly went into his house and returned with two dowsing rods made out of metal coat hangers. He proceeded to dowse the exact location of the buried line before placing the posts. I was surprised he knew how to dowse and that he seemed so confident that dowsing would confirm the actual location of the water pipe. And, it did.

Another incident that captured my attention occurred at the college where I worked. A new building project there required excavation near a buried electrical line. The electric company sent a man out to mark the line's location by using an electronic detector.

Shortly after this, I observed the college's maintenance superintendent go outside and dowse the electrical line's location himself. Based on his dowsing results the superintendent told the excavators that they were likely to sever the line if they used the electric company's markings. To no avail, the excavators ignored the superintendent's warning and consequently sliced through the electrical line.

Yet in another occurrence regarding dowsing, an old friend of mine told me about how he toured the ancient sites of Mexico for a year with the personal secretary of J. Paul Getty, the oil billionaire. According to Getty's secretary, Getty paid dowsers to dowse for the locations of every oil well he drilled. To my way of thinking, what worked so well for this oil billionaire just might prove useful for my own purposes as well.

This story about Getty triggered memory of a psychic reading given to me in 1973. The psychic told me that I would eventually discover a way of receiving useful information quickly but emphasized that I should not let anyone know how I was getting the information.

At the time, I did not know why such a precaution had been given to me. I now believe the psychic was referring to my introduction to dowsing. It was not until much later on that I realized why I received such a warning.

Dowsing Outside the Box

Shortly after hearing the J. Paul Getty story, John Price, a retiree from a nearby town, walked into the college where I then worked, introduced himself and unexpectedly started talking about dowsing. As he explained dowsing and how dowsers could find water, oil and other buried objects, I began to wonder if a goat, "yours truly", could use dowsing to help me in my work.

Just maybe dowsing was my answer to getting information quickly. Like on the job and in the privacy of my own office, I could become an "information sleuth." Behind closed doors, of course! I didn't want the "institution of higher learning" where I was employed to think about sending me to another "institution." Smile.

So I asked John, "Have you heard of anyone using dowsing to develop grant proposals before they are submitted to funding agencies?" He replied, "No, that's really different, Jim! However, there are dowsers with other specialized interests. Within the membership of the American Society of Dowsers, there are dowsers who specialize in such areas as finding water, oil, gas, minerals, buried treasure, missing persons and escaped criminals, but I have never heard of anyone using dowsing to make decisions about grant proposals."

As a founding dean of a corporate and community service's division at the college, I was to develop proposals, design new projects and generate funding to support those efforts. Every proposal and project was different and often involved multiple funding streams. I was already receiving information from my dreams that had proved useful for my work but I now needed to obtain guidance in a more timely fashion throughout my workday.

I couldn't just go to sleep on the job to receive dream information like Thomas Edison did. Unlike Edison, who owned his own invention laboratory, civil servants seldom have on-the-job sleeping rights written into their job descriptions. I needed another method of getting information.

Pendulum Dowsing

I decided to use pendulum dowsing in my work. The pendulum is relatively small, portable and easy to use. A pendulum looks much like a pull cord for a ceiling fan. It has a chain, cord or string with a weighted object hanging from one end of the chain, cord or string. In fact, pull cords make good pendulums even though they are usually somewhat larger than your standard pendulums. Car or truck keys on a knotted cord work equally as well and don't take up much room in one's pocket or purse.

Using the pendulum allowed me to dowse discretely without raising a whole lot of questions from those who might be unfamiliar with or opposed to dowsing.

I won't go into too much detail about how to dowse with a pendulum, except to briefly describe how it is used. Similar to pre-sleep suggestions, you use affirmations prior to asking your dowsing question. Then you simply hold the pendulum at the top of the chain or cord and allow the suspended object to hang freely. Start with the pendulum hanging in a stationary position and wait until the pendulum starts to swing in a particular direction.

Initially, I started with just a simple dowsing process; a vertical swing meant a "yes answer" and a horizontal swing indicated a "no answer." Later on, I used a diagonal swing to my right to show me that it was "not time yet" for that question's possible answer. A diagonal swing to my left meant I should "amend or rephrase my question."

There are many ways to pattern and improve your pendulum questions and overall dowsing techniques. The samples given above are only to serve as examples of possible ways to use a pendulum in dowsing for answers.

There are oodles of books out there with elaborate charts that allow for many different swings and hundreds of possible answers with pendulum dowsing.* The books can acquaint you with affirmations and help you develop and ask appropriate, clear and concise questions to insure better results from your dowsing.

Connecting with Unique Individuals

John Price, the retiree I had met, invited me to go with him and his friends to an Annual Convention and School of the American Society of Dowsers held then in Danville, Vermont.

We stayed at a rented cottage on Indian Joe's Pond. What an adventure I had! One of John's friends turned out to be a previous president of the American Society of Dowsers and another friend, staying with us, became president the following year! These master dowsers filled our evenings there with amazing stories of their latest

---

* The American Society of Dowsers" online bookstore has an excellent supply of dowsing books and devices such as pendulums. Used dowsing books are available online at a substantial discount at sites like Abebook, Alibris and Amazon.com.

pursuits, experiences and discoveries. John took me under his wing and introduced me to some of the finest dowsers that I was ever to meet. And, I was hoping their dowsing abilities would rub off on me.

While at the conference, my dowsing was more accurate and I believe this was because I was in the aura, the thought form and the energy field of these great dowsers. Unfortunately, when I got back home my dowsing accuracy nose-dived. I became disheartened because my dowsing was not yet as accurate as I had initially hoped it would be.

A personal confession is in order here. If I had been meditating regularly as Nan Moore had advised, I do believe that my dowsing accuracy would have increased much faster than it did.

Skill Development

The following summer some of my friends and I went to a small dowsing conference in Illinois. By then, I was very discouraged with my dowsing results. While at the conference, a successful oil dowser told me about his initial lack of success with dowsing. He further related that he had to practice dowsing for two years before getting accurate and reliable results from his dowsing.

After first having very little success with his dowsing, he developed a simple but effective plan to increase his accuracy. He acquired a bucket full of fresh crude oil from an oil field. He lived in a two-story house and would go upstairs and wait until his daughter had secretly placed the sealed bucket of oil in one of the downstairs rooms.

He would stay upstairs, dowse and try to pinpoint the exact location of the crude oil that was placed somewhere on the first floor below. He only considered his dowsing a success if, while upstairs, he ended up standing right over the exact location of the crude oil on the floor below.

Again, it took him two years, but he later became a very successful oil dowser. His story and persistence inspired me to continue dowsing until I could obtain reliable results with my pendulum dowsing.

Taking Dowsing to Work

Alas, in time, my own dowsing did improve. I started using dowsing to cut through the complexities of my work. Part of my job was the startup of new projects and related proposals and grants. The rural area my college served needed jobs; so I concentrated on county, state and federal workforce development proposals and grant funding in hopes of bringing jobs to that region.

Grants and funding sources would come and go and the writing of such was time consuming. I used dowsing to determine if I had a winning concept or proposal, *before its actual submission to funding agencies.* If not, I would dowse and modify aspects of the proposal that needed changed to create a successful grant proposal.

All but one grant of the many I submitted received approval and funding. This one, a large state grant to build a workforce development center, was compromised at the county level. Even a state senator had difficulty changing the minds of the individuals involved. It never occurred to me that such a thing would influence the outcome of my submission or that there was a need to dowse for such an eventuality.

After losing the grant mentioned above, I started dowsing how best to promote projects, individually, to the president and board of trustees at the college and the movers and shakers within the region.

The help I received from non-physical realms, dreams and dowsing helped keep a growing staff employed and provided much needed services for thousands in our region. Throughout this effort, we seldom used traditional forms of advertising and marketing. Yet, we had more work coming to our door than we could handle.

Finding Your Own Way

Guidance is available to us through our higher selves, angels, guides, prophets, seers and so on. It is crucial that we develop better ways to receive and discern the information that comes to us. Dowsing is yet another method to receive guidance from a higher source.

We can access information about almost anything through dowsing, not just water, precious stones, minerals, oil and the like. With dowsing, we can receive answers to any questions posed—as long as we are not invading the privacy of others or using dowsing for harmful purposes.

Learning to dowse can give us a definite edge in life and we can develop an uncanny ability to navigate through life's difficulties and maximize the best of our opportunities.

Throughout the course of our life, we will make many decisions. The better our decision-making, the better the quality of our lives can become. As we learn to trust the guidance we receive through dowsing, we can lessen the uncertainty we feel, become more decisive and move on with our lives.

Nan Moore, author of this book, not only suggests that we choose and develop a method of receiving our own information from our higher self but that we also establish a practice of meditating on a daily basis. This, she says, will further enhance our ability to receive guidance.

In addition, it is especially important that we pass on the knowledge we receive to the next generation. Edward (Terry) Ross, the founder and one time president of the American Society of Dowsers once said, "If we would teach our children how to dowse, no one could ever tell them an untruth!"

© Fitzwilliam Museum, Cambridge

11

LOOK UP!

(CONCLUDING VISION AND PRAYER)

> "Angels take different forms at the bidding of their master, God, and thus reveal themselves to men and unveil the divine mysteries to them." [1] *Saint John of Damascus*

When you are out at night, don't you sometimes look up at the stars and wonder about the things that you see? You might ask yourself, "Was that an airplane off in the distance or could it be a UFO?"

Some people say that visitors have already come to the Earth in unidentified flying objects, (UFOs). Many of the less evolved public might scoff when they hear about UFOs, choosing not to believe such is possible, even though we have sent humans aboard spacecrafts to the moon. In spite of public ridicule, reports of UFO sightings and evidence of UFOs have persisted throughout the ages, such as:

In the 1710 painting of the Baptism of Christ, by Flemish artist, Aert van Gelder [2] (shown to the left), is what appears to be a UFO-like object in the sky.

In yet another 1486 painting titled, The Annunciation with Saint Emidius [3] by Carlo Crivelli, there appears to be a saucer-shaped cloud with a shaft of light beaming down to a building. "Perhaps the earliest UFO sightings occurred in 1450 B.C., when Egyptians saw bright circles of light in the sky." [4]

According to my spirit guides, our planet has had many visitors from ancient times to present. Our higher self knows UFO's exist and that there are other life forms out there.

For some time now psychics, prophets and even our scientists have given numerous warnings about the destructive path humanity is taking. It is imperative that we change our way of thinking and treating each other, the Earth and its other life forms. It may be that when the Earth begins to shake and more and more cataclysmic things begin to befall us, we will think the end of the world is coming.

I believe the world will not end, but it will change and it will not be as it is today. When it seems as if we are doomed—we begin to sense something good is about to happen and we look upward and we see many, many spaceships coming.

As they get closer and closer, we will begin to remember them, what they can do and we will be elated. The spaceships contain Avatars and they know how to use and balance energy in a benevolent manner.*

They are beings of love with much knowledge. Their compassion will have a profound effect upon us. We will love them. And, as they begin to move among us, we will remember that they have been here before. We will know that they can help us.

---

* This visit by Avatars to Earth does not involve in any way, shape, form or fashion—the extraterrestrials known as the "Grays."

Some of these advanced beings will help us balance energy and bring peace and harmony to the planet. Others will talk with us instilling knowledge, love, compassion, mercy and forgiveness. They will teach us for a while but then it will be time for the Avatars to leave.

At that time, we will become sad. We will not want them to go but they have to. We have more lessons to learn and teach. As these Avatars move away from the Earth again, our memories of them and their visit will dim and, finally, there will be no conscious memory of them. Like before, we will continue to look up at the stars and wonder—are there other life forms out there?

The Avatars did their job. Now, it is up to us! Will we fall back into the negative path of destruction, hate and greed? Only time will tell.

🕊 Concluding Prayer

May the blessings of God and Spirit be showered upon us like the rains of spring, fertilizing the spiritual seeds planted in our souls, so that we may go forth and gain more and greater knowledge regarding life here and hereafter. May we share that knowledge with our fellow humans until all can say in the name of truth, Amen!

REFLECTIONS AND ADDENDUM

By Nan Moore

There are scriptures from the Bible that deal with casting out evil spirits, clairaudience, clairvoyance, differing gifts, dreams, healing, materialization, physical psychic phenomena, promise of vision, prophecy, recorded spirit lights, reincarnation, spirit writing, trance, visions and many other amazing extraordinary happenings.

To me, Moses was a medium—a vehicle through which the energy from highly evolved entities brought knowledge to him and prophesied through him. Moses received the Ten Commandments on tablets of stone; the commandments were Spirit writings transmitted through him.

Not many in that time had evolved to the point they could tolerate the higher vibrations as Moses did. Yet, they could act as a receiver, from Spirit, of information that dealt with issues not as important as universal laws, commandments or spiritual truths.

Spirit conveyed to me that not everything in the Bible is true. Men wrote the Bible using the level of their understanding at the time they wrote it. Reliable evidence exists today that details how men changed parts of the Bible according to their own belief system.

God inspired the Bible, but man wrote it. If people are not at the level of awareness to discern truth, then the passages would go right over their head and they could do nothing else except take what they have read, literally. However, many truths remain in the Bible whose meanings are yet to be revealed to those who seek a greater understanding.

In the Addendum that follows are scriptural quotes from the King James Version of the Bible[1]. It was not my intention to pull passages from the Bible out of context. I felt that the gist of the following quotes and passages parallel the book's chapter and subchapter topics and points nicely. I encourage you to search the scriptures and meditate on verses that resonate with your higher self and discover for yourself what the following scriptures reveal to you, personally:

ADDENDUM

"But the wisdom that is from above is first pure, then peaceable, gentle, and easy to be intreated, full of mercy and good fruits, without partiality, and without hypocrisy."   James 3:17, p 1650

CHAPTER 1 - GIFTS

Psychic Gifts

"But all these worketh that one and the selfsame Spirit, dividing to every man severally as he will."   1 Corinthians 12:11, p 1563

At First Sight and Sound

"Then the eyes of the blind shall be opened, and the ears of the deaf shall be unstopped."   Isaiah 35:5, p 988

We Shall See What We Shall See

"For the prophecy came not in old time by the will of man: but holy men of God spake as they *were* moved by the Holy Ghost."
                    2 Peter 1:21, p 1660

CHAPTER 1 - GIFTS

My First Reading

"Now there are diversities of gifts, but the same Spirit. And there are differences of administrations . . . And there are diversities of operations, but it is the same God which worketh all in all." 1 Corinthians 12:4-6, p 1563

No True End in Sight

"I am he that liveth, and was dead; and behold, I am alive for evermore . . ."
Revelation 1:18, p 1674

CHAPTER 2 - GIFT EVOLUTION

The Search for Truth

"Howbeit when he, the Spirit of truth, is come, he will guide you into all truth: for he shall not speak of himself; but whatsoever he shall hear, *that* shall he speak: and he will shew you things to come."

John 16:13, p 1466

Meditation—My Foundation

"Be still, and know that I am God: I will be exalted among the heathen, I will be exalted in the earth."   Psalm 46:10, p 826

"Then are they glad because they be quiet; so he bringeth them unto their desired haven."   Psalm 107:30, p 871

"And be renewed in the spirit of your mind; And that ye put on the new man . . ."   Ephesians 4:23-24, p 1595

Psychometry

"But covet earnestly the best gifts: and yet shew I unto you a more excellent way."   1 Corinthians 12:31, p 1564

Be Careful What You Ask For

"Likewise the Spirit also helpeth our infirmities: for we know not what we should pray for as we ought: but the Spirit itself maketh intercession for us with groanings which cannot be uttered."   Romans 8:26, p 1538

Criminal Cases and Missing Persons

"But let none of you suffer as a murderer, or as a thief, or as an evildoer . . ."

1 Peter 4:15, p 1657

Spirit Mentor—Channeling

"(Before time in Israel, when a man went to enquire of God, thus he spake, Come, and let us go to the seer: for *he that is* now called a Prophet was beforetime called a Seer.)"   1 Samuel 9:9, p 420

"For ye may all prophesy one by one, that all may learn, and all may be comforted. And the spirits of the prophets are subject to the prophets."

1 Corinthians 14:31-32, p 1566

CHAPTER 2 - GIFT EVOLUTION

Going a Different Direction

"No man has seen God at anytime. If we love one another, God dwelleth in us, and his love is perfected in us."   I John 4:12, p 1666

"A new heart also will I give you, and a new spirit will I put within you: and I will take away the stony heart out of your flesh, and I give you an heart of flesh. And I will put my spirit within you, and cause you to walk in my statues, and ye shall keep my judgments, and do them."
                                                        Ezekiel 36:26-27, p 1177

An Angel Appears

"Let brotherly love continue. Be not forgetful to entertain strangers: for thereby some have entertained angels unawares."
                                                        Hebrews 13:1-2, p 1645

"Behold, I send an Angel before thee, to keep thee in the way, and to bring thee into the place which I have prepared."   Exodus 23:20, p 116

CHAPTER 3 - EVOLUTION AND SOUL MEMORY

Angels Go Astray

"All we like sheep have gone astray; we have turned every one to his own way . . ."
                                                        Isaiah 53:6, p 1011

The Path of the Soul

"And as we have borne the image of the earthly, we shall also bear the image of the heavenly."
                                                        1 Corinthians 15:49, p 1568

Shape Shifting

"It is sown a natural body; it is raised a spiritual body. There is a natural body, and there is a spiritual body."
                                                        1 Corinthians 15:44, p 1568

"Ye are our epistle written in our hearts, known and read of all men . . . written not with ink, but with the Spirit of the living God; not in tables of stone, but in fleshly tables of the heart."
                                                        2 Corinthians 3:2-3, p 1572

"The law of the Lord is perfect, converting the soul: the testimony of the Lord is sure, making wise the simple."
                                                        Psalm 19:7, p 807

Earthbound Spirits

"Beloved, believe not every spirit, but try the spirits whether they are of God: because many false prophets are gone out into the world."
                                                        1 John 4:1, p 1666

Death and Grieving

"Blessed are they that mourn: for they shall be comforted."
                                                        Matthew 5:4, p 1301

CHAPTER 4 - ENERGY AND SPIRIT

Universal Laws and Principles

"The secret things belong unto the Lord our God: but those things which are revealed belong unto us and to our children for ever, that we may do all the words of this law."   Deuteronomy 29:29, p 315

"And I will give unto thee the keys of the kingdom of heaven: and whatsoever thou shalt bind on earth shall be bound in heaven: and whatsoever thou shalt loose on earth shall be loosed in heaven."   Matthew 16:19, p 1323

Energy and Spirit

"The wind bloweth where it listeth, and thou hearest the sound thereof, but canst not tell whence it cometh, and whither it goeth: so is every one that is born of the Spirit."   John 3:8, p 1439

"Through faith we understand that the worlds were framed by the word of God, so that things which are seen were not made of things which do appear."   Hebrews 11:3, p 1641

Feminine and Masculine Energy

"So God created man in his own image, in the image of God created he him; male and female created he them."   Genesis 1:27, p 2

God

"God is a Spirit: and they that worship him must worship him in spirit and in truth."   John 4:24, p 1442

"Hereby know we that we dwell in him, and he in us, because he hath given us of his Spirit."   1 John 4:13, p 1666

"He that loveth not knoweth not God; for God is love."   1 John 4:8, p 1666

"For by him were all things created, that are in heaven, and that are in earth, visible and invisible, whether they be thrones, or dominions, or principalities, or powers: all things were created by him, and for him: And he is before all things, and by him all things consist."   Colossians 1:16-17, p 1603

Chapter 4 - ENERGY AND SPIRIT

No Hell?

"If I ascend up to into heaven, thou art there: If I make my bed in hell, behold, thou art there. If I take the wings of the morning, and dwell in the uttermost parts of the sea; Even there shall thy hand lead me, and thy right hand shall hold me."
                                          Psalm 139:8-10, p 891

"For I am persuaded, that neither death, nor life, nor angels, nor principalities, nor powers, nor things present, nor things to come, Nor height, nor depth, nor any other creature, shall be able to separate us from the love of God . . ."
                                          Romans 8:38-39, p 1539

"For I know the thoughts that I think toward you, saith the Lord, thoughts of peace, and not of evil, to give you an expected end."
                                          Jeremiah 29:11, p 1069

"For the Father judgeth no man, but hath committed all judgment unto the Son . . ."
                                          John 5:22, p 1444

Death—The Transition

"While we look not at the things which are seen, but at the things which are not seen: for the things which are seen are temporal; but the things which are not seen are eternal."
                                          2 Corinthians 4:18, p 1573

"For this corruptible must put on incorruption, and this mortal must put on immortality."
                                          1 Corinthians 15:53, p 1568

". . . A man can receive nothing, except it be given him from heaven."
                                          John 3:27, p 1440

"And the foundations of the wall of the city were garnished with all manner of precious stones . . . And the twelve gates were twelve pearls . . . and the street of the city was pure gold, as it were transparent glass."
                                          Revelation 21:19-21, p 1695-96

CHAPTER 5 - REINCARNATION

The Soul Reborn

"And no man hath ascended up to heaven, but he that came down from heaven, even the Son of man which is in heaven."   John 3:13, p 1439

"Marvel not that I said unto thee, Ye must be born again."
John 3:7, p 1439

"The Lord shall preserve thy going out and thy coming in from this time forth, and even for evermore."   Psalm 121:8, p 884

"For if a man think himself to be something, when he is nothing, he deceives himself."   Galatians 6:3, p 1590

Soul Mates and Friends

"For where your treasure is, there will your heart be also."
Matthew 6:21, p 1304

"And above all these things *put on* charity, which is the bond of perfectness."
Colossians 3:14, p 1606

My Son, Tony

"Thou shalt not kill."   Exodus 20:13, p 111

". . . Suffer little children, and forbid them not, to come unto me: for of such is the kingdom of heaven."   Mathew 19:14, p 1327

Mother Mary and a Rose

"As one whom his mother comforteth, so I will comfort you . . . And when ye see this, your heart shall rejoice . . ."   Isaiah 66:13-14, p 1024-25

"And Mary said, Behold the handmaid of the Lord; be it unto me according to thy word. And the angel departed from her."
Luke 1:38, p 1382

CHAPTER 6 - KARMA, FORGIVENESS AND SOUL MEMORIES

Cause and Effect

"As we have therefore opportunity, let us do good unto all men . . ."
Galatians 6:10, p 1590

"And let us not be weary in well doing: for in due season we shall reap, if we faint not."
Galatians 6:9, p 1590

". . . as thou hast done, it shall be done unto thee: thy reward shall return upon thine own head."
Obadiah Verse 15, p 1250

"Judge not, that ye be not judged. For with what judgment ye judge, ye shall be judged: and with what measure ye mete, it shall be measured to you again."
Matthew 7:1-2, p 1305

"But if ye bite and devour one another, take heed that ye be not consumed one of another."
Galatians 5:15, p 1589

Forgiveness

"And forgive us our sins; for we also forgive every one that is indebted to us . . ."
Luke 11:4, p 1406

". . . Lord, how oft shall my brother sin against me, and I forgive him? till seven times? Jesus saith unto him, "I say not unto thee, Until seven times: but, Until seventy times seven."
Matthew 18:21-22, p 1326

Remembering Past Lives

"Remember the days of old, consider the years of many generations . . ."
Deuteronomy 32:7, p 319

"But I say unto to you, That Elias is come already, and they knew him not . . ."
Matthew 17:12, p 1324

Soul Memory and Future Planning

"Hast thou not heard long ago, how I have done it; and of ancient times, that I have formed it? now have I brought it to pass . . ."
Isaiah 37:26, p 991

CHAPTER 7 - FEAR AND SOUL MEMORIES

Fear Memories

"For the thing which I greatly feared is come upon me, and that which I was afraid of is come unto me."   Job 3:25, p 759

". . . Let not your hearts be troubled, neither let it be afraid."
                                        John 14:27, p 1464

Releasing Fear Memories

"Say to them that are of a fearful heart, Be strong, fear not: behold, your God will come with vengeance, even God with a recompence: he will come and save you."   Isaiah 35:4, p 988

"There is no fear in love; but perfect love casteth out fear: because fear hath torment. He that feareth is not make perfect in love."
                                        1 John 4:18, p 1667

"But let him ask in faith, nothing wavering. For he that wavereth is like a wave of the sea driven with the wind and tossed."   James 1:6, p 1647

CHAPTER 8 - WHY PEOPLE ARE HOMOSEXUAL

"Whosoever hateth his brother is a murderer: and ye know that no murderer hath eternal life abiding in him."   1 John 3:15, p 1665

"Let us not therefore judge one another any more: but judge this rather, that no man put a stumbling block or an occasion to fall in his brother's way."
Romans 14:13, p 1546

How Past Incarnations Form a Heterosexual Nature

" . . . and on the side of their oppressors there was power; but they had no comforter."   Ecclesiastes 4:1, p 935

"Love worketh no ill to his neighbor . . ."   Romans 13:10, p 1545

How Past Incarnations Form a Homosexual Nature

". . . and considered all the oppressions that are done under the sun: and behold the tears of such as were oppressed, and they had no comforter. . ."
Ecclesiastes 4:1, p 935

". . . therefore love is the fulfilling of the law." Romans 13:10, p 1545

The Ultimate Conscientious Objectors

"Ye have heard that it was said by them of old time, THOU SHALL NOT KILL; and whosoever shall kill shall be in danger of the judgment."
Matthew 5:21, p 1302

Wounding the Spirit

" . . . hearken unto my speech: for I have slain a man to my wounding, and a young man to my hurt."   Genesis 4:23, p 6

"The Lord is nigh unto them that are of a broken heart; and saveth such as be of a contrite spirit."   Psalm 34:18, p 817

The Peacemakers

"Peace I leave with you, my peace I give unto you: not as the world giveth, give I unto you . . ."   John 14:27, p 1464

CHAPTER 8 - WHY PEOPLE ARE HOMOSEXUAL

The Peacemakers (continued)

"Let us therefore follow after the things which make for peace, and things wherewith one may edify another."   Romans 14:19, p 1546

Cause and Effect Energy Variations

"For as he thinketh in his heart, so is he . . ."

Proverbs 23:7, p 921

CHAPTER 9 - RECEIVING GUIDANCE THROUGH DREAMS

"And he said, Hear now my words: If there be a prophet among you, I the Lord will make myself known unto him in a vision, and will speak unto him in a dream."
                                                    Numbers 12:6, p 222

"And it shall come to pass afterward, that I will pour out my spirit upon all flesh; and your sons and your daughters shall prophesy, your old men shall dream dreams, your young men shall see visions: And also upon the servants and upon the handmaids in those days I pour out my spirit."
                                                    Joel 2:28-29, p 1237

"I saw in the night visions, and, behold, one like the Son of man came with the clouds of heaven, and came to the Ancient of days, and they brought him near before him."
                                                    Daniel 7:13, 1214

Rediscovering the Importance of Dreams

"In a dream, in a vision of the night, when deep sleep falleth upon men, in slumbering upon the bed; Then he openeth the ears of men, and sealeth their instruction, That he may withdraw man from his purpose, and hide pride from man."
                                                    Job 33:15-17, p 786

How Dreams Became Important to Me

"Prove all things; hold fast that which is good."
                                                    1 Thessalonians 5:21, 1611

"For if there be first a willing mind, it is accepted according to that a man hath, and not according to that he hath not."   2 Corinthians 8:12, p 1577

Using Dreams to Find a Date or Mate

"For where your treasure is, there will your heart be also."
                                                    Matthew 6:21, 1304

"By a new and living way, which he hath consecrated for us, through the veil, that is to say, his flesh . . . "   Hebrews 10:20, 1640

"They have not known nor understood: for he hath shut their eyes, that they cannot see; and their hearts, that they cannot understand."
                                                    Isaiah 44:18, 1001

CHAPTER 9 - RECEIVING GUIDANCE THROUGH DREAMS

Heeding Warning Dreams and Changing the Future!

"For he shall give his angels charge over thee, to keep thee in all thy ways."
Psalm 91:11, p 859

"Daniel answered in the presence of the king, and said, The secret which the king hath demanded cannot the wise men, the astrologers, the magicians, the soothsayers, shew unto the king; But there is a God in heaven that revealeth secrets, and maketh known to the king Nebuchadnezzar what shall be in the latter days. Thy dream, and the visions of thy head upon thy bed, are these . . ."
Daniel 2:27-28, p 1202-03

"And Joseph dreamed a dream, and he told it his brethren: and they hated him yet the more. And he said unto them, Hear, I pray you, this dream which I have dreamed . . ."
Genesis 37:5-6, p 56

"But while he thought on these things, behold, the angel of the Lord appeared unto him in a dream, saying, Joseph, thou son of David, fear not to take unto thee Mary thy wife: for that which is conceived in her is of the Holy Ghost."
Matthew 1:20, p 1297-98

"And being warned of God in a dream that they should not return to Herod, they departed into their own country another way."
Matthew 2:12, p 1298

"In the first year of Belshazzar, king of Babylon, Daniel had a dream and visions of his head upon his bed: then he wrote the dream, and told the sum of the matters."
Daniel 7:1, p 1213

"And they dreamed a dream both of them, each man his dream in one night, each man according to the interpretation of his dream . . ."
Genesis 40:5, p 61

"And they said unto him, We have dreamed a dream, and there is no interpreter of it. And Joseph said unto them, Do not interpretations belong to God? Tell me them, I pray you."
Genesis 40:8, p 61

"AWAKE THOU THAT SLEEPEST, AND ARISE FROM THE DEAD, AND CHRIST SHALL GIVE THE LIGHT."
Ephesians 5:14, p 1596

Enriching Your Life

"But as it is written, EYE HATH NOT SEEN, NOR EAR HEARD, NEITHER HAVE ENTERED INTO THE HEART OF MAN, THE THINGS WHICH GOD HATH PREPARED FOR THEM THAT LOVE HIM."
1 Corinthians 2:9, p 1551

Chapter 10 - ACCESSING INFORMATION THROUGH DOWSING

"And he removed from thence, and digged another well; and for that they strove not . . . For now the Lord hath made room for us, and we shall be fruitful in the land."
                                                                                Genesis 26:21-22, p 37

"And the Lord said unto Moses, Go on before the people, and take with thee of the elders of Israel; and thy rod, wherewith thou smotest the river, take in thine hand, and go. Behold, I will stand before thee there upon the rock in Horeb; and thou shalt smite the rock, and there shall come water out of it, that the people may drink. And Moses did so in the sight of the elders of Israel."
                                                                                Exodus 17:5-6, p 107

Capturing My Attention

"He that believeth . . . out of his belly shall flow rivers of living water."
                                                                                John 7:38, p 1450

Dowsing Outside the Box

"Moreover the word of the Lord came unto me, saying, Jeremiah, what seest thou? And I said, I see a rod of an almond tree. Then said the Lord unto me, Thou hast well seen: for I will hasten my word to perform it."
                                                                                Jeremiah 1:11-12, p 1026

Pendulum Dowsing

"Having then gifts differing according to the grace that is given to us, whether prophecy, let us prophesy according to the proportion of faith . . ."
                                                                                Romans 12:6, p 1544

Connecting With Unique Individuals

"Wherefore he saith, WHEN HE ASCENDED UP ON HIGH, HE LED CAPTIVITY CAPTIVE, AND GAVE GIFTS UNTO MEN."   Ephesians 4:8, p 1594

Skill Development

"But let every man prove his own work, and then shall he have rejoicing in himself alone, and not in another."   Galatians 6:4, p 1590

Taking Dowsing to Work

"For every one that asketh receiveth; and he that seeketh findeth, and to him that knocketh it shall be opened."   Matthew 7:8, p 1305

CHAPTER 10 - ACCESSING INFORMATION THROUGH DOWSING

Finding Your Own Way

"But the manifestation of the Spirit is given to every man to profit withal. For to one is given by the Spirit the word of wisdom; to another the word of knowledge by the same Spirit; to another faith by the same Spirit; to another the gifts of healing by the same Spirit; To another the working of miracles; to another prophecy; to another discerning of spirits; . . . But all these worketh that one and the selfsame Spirit, dividing to every man severally as he will."

1 Corinthians 12:7-11, p 1563

"Ye are of God, little children, and have overcome them: because greater is he that is in you, than he that is in the world."

1 John 4:4, p 1666

"And ye shall know the truth and the truth shall make you free."

John 8:32, p 1452

CHAPTER 11 - LOOK UP! (Concluding Vision and Prayer)

"And Jesus, when he was baptized . . . the heavens were opened unto him, and he saw the Spirit of God descending like a dove, and lighting upon him: And lo a voice from heaven, saying, This is my beloved son, in whom I am well pleased."

Matthew 3:16-17, p 1300

"Lift up your eyes on high and behold who hath created these *things*, that bringeth out their host by number: he calleth them all by names by the greatness of his might, for that he is strong in power; not one faileth."

Isaiah 40:26, p 995

"And I looked, and, behold, a whirlwind came out of the north, a great cloud, and a fire infolding itself, and a brightness was about it, and out of the midst thereof as the colour of amber, out of the midst of the fire."

Ezekiel 1:4, p 1121

"And when the living creatures went, the wheels went by them: and when the living creatures were lifted up from the earth, the wheels were lifted up . . . for the spirit of the living creature was in the wheels."

Ezekiel 1:19-20, p 1122

"And he saith unto him, Verily, verily, I say unto you, Hereafter ye shall see heaven open, and the angels of God ascending and descending upon the Son of man."

John 1:51, p 1438

Sources Cited

[1] THE HOLY BIBLE. King James Version, Reference Edition (Nashville, TN: Thomas Nelson Publishers, 1994), James 3:17, page 1650.

1   GIFTS

2   GIFT EVOLUTION
[1] THE HOLY BIBLE, 1 Corinthians 12:31, page 1564.
[2] THE HOLY BIBLE, Mathew 7:7, page 1305.

3   EVOLUTION AND SOUL MEMORY
[1] THE HOLY BIBLE, I Corinthians 15:44, page 1568.
[2] Ghosts, dir. Jerry Zucker, writ. Bruce Joel Rubin, perf. Patrick Swayze, Demi Moore and Whoopi Goldberg, Paramount, 1990.

4   ENERGY AND SPIRIT
[1] THE HOLY BIBLE, Mathew 28:18, page 1347.
[2] Three Initiates, Kybalion: A Study of the Hermetic Philosophy of Ancient Egypt and Greece (Chicago, IL: The Yogi Publication Society, 1908), page 30.
[3] Three Initiates, pages 28.
[4] Three Initiates, pages 32.
[5] Three I nitiates, pages 39.
[6] Three Initiates, pages 26-27.

5   REINCARNATION
[1] THE HOLY BIBLE, Psalm 121:8, page 884.
[2] THE HOLY BIBLE, 1 Corinthians 15:49, page 1568.
[3] THE HOLY BIBLE, Mathew 17:12, page 1324.
[4] THE HOLY BIBLE, John 3:7, page 1439.
[5] THE HOLY BIBLE, John 3:13, p 1439.
[6] THE HOLY BIBLE, Exodus 20:13, page 111.
[7] THE HOLY BIBLE, Mathew 19:14, page 1327.

6   KARMA, FORGIVENESS AND SOUL MEMORIES
[1] THE HOLY BIBLE, Galatians 6:9, p 1590.
[2] THE HOLY BIBLE, Obadiah Verse 15, p 1250.
[3] Three Initiates, pages 38.
[4] New Websterian 1912 Dictionary Illustrated, Syndicated Publishing Company, New York, NY, 1912, page 380.

7   FEAR AND SOUL MEMORIES
[1] THE HOLY BIBLE, I John 4:18, page 1667.

8   WHY PEOPLE ARE HOMOSEXUAL
[1] THE HOLY BIBLE, 1 John 3:15, page 1665.
[2] THE HOLY BIBLE, Romans 14:13, page 1546.

9   RECEIVING GUIDANCE THROUGH DREAMS
[1] THE HOLY BIBLE, Joel 2:28-29, p 1237.

10   ACCESSING INFORMATION THROUGH DOWSING
[1] THE HOLY BIBLE, Jeremiah 1:11-12, p 1026.

11   LOOK UP! (CONCLUDING VISION AND PRAYER)
[1] Saint John of Damascene, Book II Chapter III "Concerning Angels", An Exact Exposition of the Orthodox Faith by Saint John.
[2] Aert van Gelder, "Baptism of Christ" (circa, 1710), Fitzwilliam Museum, Cambridge, Great Britain.
[3] Carlo Crivelli, "The Annunciation with Saint Emidius", (1486), The National Gallery, London, Great Britain, http://www.nationalgallery. org.uk/painting/carlo-crivelli-the-annuncia...
[4] Jason Stahl, "20 Things You Didn't Know About Aliens," Discover, January 2007, page 80.

REFLECTIONS AND ADDENDUM

[1] THE HOLY BIBLE, Chapter, Verse, and Page(s):

James 3:17, p 1650

CHAPTER 1 — GIFTS
1 Corinthians 12:11, p 1563
Isaiah 35:5, p 988
2 Peter 1:21, p 1660
1 Corinthians 12:4-6, p 1563
Revelation 1:18, p 1674

CHAPTER 2 - GIFT EVOLUTION
John 16:13, p 1466
Psalm 46:10, p 826
Psalm 107:30, p 871
Ephesians 4:23-24, p 1595
1 Corinthians 12:31, p 1564
Romans 8:26, p 1538
1 Peter 4:15, p 1657
1 Samuel 9:9, p 420
1 Corinthians 14:31-32, p 1566
I John 4:12, p 1666
Ezekiel 36:26-27, p 1177
Hebrews 13:1-2, p 1645
Exodus 23:20, p 116

CHAPTER 3 - EVOLUTION AND SOUL MEMORY

Isaiah 53:6, p 1011
1 Corinthians 15:49, p 1568
1 Corinthians 15:44, p 1568
2 Corinthians 3:2-3, p 1572
Psalm 19:7, p 807
1 John 4:1, p 1666
Matthew 5:4, p 1301

CHAPTER 4 - ENERGY AND SPIRIT

Deuteronomy 29:29, p 315
Matthew 16:19, p 1323
John 3:8, p 1439
Hebrews 11:3, p 1641
Genesis 1:27, p 2
John 4:24, p 1442
1 John 4:13, p 1666
1 John 4:8, p 1666
Colossians 1:16-17, p 1603
Psalm 139:8-10, p 891
Romans 8:38-39, p 1539
Jeremiah 29:11, p 1069
John 5:22, p 1444
2 Corinthians 4:18, p 1573
1 Corinthians 15:53, p 1568
John 3:27, p 1440
Revelation 21:19-21, p 1695-96

CHAPTER 5 – REINCARNATION

John 3:13, p 1439
John 3:7, p 1439
Psalm 121:8, p 884
Galatians 6:3, p 1590
Matthew 6:21, p 1304
Colossians 3:14, p 1606
Exodus 20:13, p 111
Mathew 19:14, p 1327
Isaiah 66:13-14, p 1024-25
Luke 1:38, p 1382

TEXT BOX WORDS AND DEFINITIONS [as noted] TAKEN FROM:

[1]New Websterian 1912 Dictionary Illustrated, Syndicated Publishing Company, New York, NY, 1912.

[Chapter 2, p 8]
psychical   pertaining to, or connected with, the human soul, spirit; or mind; spiritualistic; psychological. Also psychic
New Websterian, p 659

[Chapter 2, p 8]
intuition   instinctive knowledge or feeling; immediate perception
New Websterian, p 467

[Chapter 3, p 24]
evolution   development or growth; the gradual development or descent of forms of life from simple or low organized types consisting of a single cell
New Websterian, p 305

[Chapter 3, p 24]
creation   the act of creating; the thing created; the universe
New Websterian, p 216

[Chapter 3, p 26]
soul   spiritual, rational, and immortal part in man; reason or intellect; conscience; life; essence; moving or inspiring power
New Websterian, p 771

[Chapter 3, p 28]
ghost   the spirit of a deceased person; apparition; the soul; breath of life; shadow
New Websterian, p 370

[Chapter 4, p 36]
energy   internal or inherent power; vigorous operation; power efficiently and forcibly exerted
New Websterian, p 293

[Chapter 4, p 44]
charity   the disposition to think well of others; liberality; alms; universal love
New Websterian, p 167

TEXT BOX WORDS AND DEFINITIONS (continued):

[Chapter 5, p 52]
Reincarnation   a return to body and flesh, after having left them for a more spiritual state. The possibility of Reincarnation is held by the Christians as well as by the Brahmans. [Latin]
New Websterian, p 689

[Chapter 5, p 52}
Incarnation   the act of clothing with, or of assuming, flesh; embodiment in human form; a striking exemplification or personification; the assumption of human nature by the Son of God [Latin}   New Websterian, p 444

[Chapter 6, p 68]
forgiveness   pardon; remission   New Websterian, p 346

[Chapter 7, p 80]
fear   apprehension of evil or danger; dread; anxiety
New Websterian, p 321

About the Author,
Nan Moore

Nan Moore, at a very young age, realized that her mother and grandmother possessed special abilities and that their family homes appeared "haunted." Further, that musical ghosts played the piano very late at night, strange guests materialized then disappeared and small objects moved seemingly on their own, all quite unexpectedly. No one would or could explain to her why these things were happening. Oddly enough, she was the only one in her family not put off by these extraordinary events.

Determined to find her own answers, at a very young age she ventured out to have her fortune read. At the reading, she had a consciousness-altering experience of seeing her beloved (then deceased) grandfather appear before her. The event so changed her reality that she has devoted the rest of her life exploring the world of Spirit. What she encountered held her interest, astonished and bewildered her, yet commanded her attention for decades.

Her journey has taken her from truth seeker as a child and teenager to wife, mother, metaphysical student, psychic, teacher, ordained minister and finally to author of this book. In addition, she successfully collaborated with law enforcement in five different states to find missing persons and solve criminal cases.

Fortunately, Nan Moore has chosen to commit to paper, the richness of all her experiences in this book and to communicate what she has seen, heard and sensed about the non-physical world.

Acknowledgements
Nan Moore

My book isn't very big in regards to the number of pages but it is one of my biggest endeavors ever.

I want to thank James for giving in to my pleading to write the chapters on dreams and dowsing. He has so much expertise in these areas—a lot more than what he has written. He has spent many, many (probably lifetimes, too) years searching, asking and receiving. I am sure he has a book in him that may come out someday—Good work, James!

I also want to thank LU for transcription, typing, graphic layout and editing the book. LU would come up with some very good advice to make things flow more smoothly and I appreciate that.

To sum it up, this book would never have gotten this far had it not been for James and LU.

Thank God and God bless.

www.ingramcontent.com/pod-product-compliance
Lightning Source LLC
Chambersburg PA
CBHW080049280326
41934CB00014B/3255